Scarlett the Pig

Steve Howell

Based on a true story

Illustrated by Alan Jones

Scarlett the Pig

First published in 2017

Stephen Howell

Copyright © Stephen Howell, 2017

ISBN 978-1542477833

DEDICATION

To my father who was my role model through life. Everyone who met him loved his company. Arthur loved a good debate plus a good game of chess; sorry I was never able to give you a great game.

Thank you Dad, for all the fun times we had together. You're missed every day. You never know, you might be able to see it in the after-life.

Mmmm, bet you're shaking your head as you read thinking, 'Yep, that's my boy'!

.

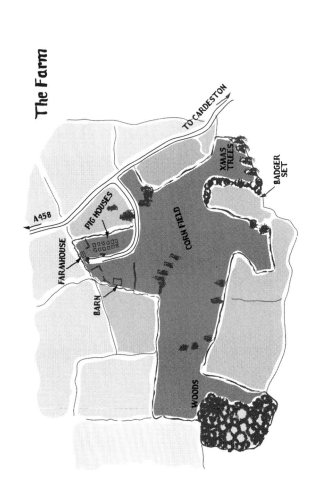

The Farm

TO CARDESTON

A458

PIG HOUSES

FARMHOUSE

BARN

CORN FIELD

XMAS TREES

BADGER SET

WOODS

CHAPTER 1
NANNY MCPHEE

My name is Stephen, but everyone calls me Steve. I am forty-four. I am a property developer and have been self-employed for a few years now. I am of slim build and I will always have a go at anything, but that is not always a good idea as I don't really think things through before I attempt them. My daughter is called Alexandra; everyone calls her Alex, and she is nearly nine going on twenty. Alex has been in private education since she was three. A bright, good looking girl, slim, with long brown hair and a great sense of humour and she laughs at what her dad gets up to. We are the best of friends and always get along, never falling out, always enjoying each other's company.

We are standing on the red carpet at Leicester Square in London, waiting for Emma Thompson to arrive, the star of

Nanny McPhee and the Big Bang. Why are we standing here, you may be thinking. Well we are not alone; sitting at our feet is a very special pig called Scarlett, who has all the cameras fixed on her. She is just sitting there taking it all in her stride. Scarlett has a beautiful harness on, which is red with lots of diamonds on it, oh... ok, glass. Scarlett is an unusual breed of pig. She is a Mangalitza, which is a woolly pig. She looks like a sheep but Scarlett is a pig, I call her a shig. We had arrived earlier and parked the car and pig trailer at Leicester Square car park. We had taken Scarlett for a walk. We started to walk past the door of an old fashioned sweet shop. I saw Scarlett looking into the shop. The smell of the sweets coming out of the shop was amazing. The smell must have been too much and Scarlett dragged me into the shop knocking over a display stand of sherbet. Scarlett shoved her face straight into the middle of the sherbet and started to lap it up. Everyone around us was laughing, even the shop keeper who was taking photos of us. I was thinking he was doing this for the insurance, but at least he had a smile on his face. I gestured I would help out with paying for the damage but he refused and wished us well with our evening ahead.

Alex and I had time to kill so we went for a walk down towards the Houses of Parliament. We had a quick look around as we were running out of time. I took a few photos of Alex and Scarlett together. As we headed back, we went via the Horse Guards' Parade. We went to look at the Guards on their horses, not knowing that horses have a dislike for pigs. As we walked towards a horse it started to jump around and rear itself up. The Guard was trying to control it but all of a sudden the horse bolted off down the street, with the guard just being a passenger now. Alex and I looked at each other. "We had better head back quickly," I said, "before we get into any more trouble."

After this we went for a walk around Trafalgar Square, I had taken Scarlett there before on a previous visit, but more about that later. We were getting mobbed by all the Japanese tourists, complete with their cameras. As we walked her around, more and more people gathered, there must have been hundreds of people cramming around us to take a photo. Scarlett was enjoying the attention but she needed her rest. So we headed back to the car to put her in the trailer and let her rest before her big night.

So here we are a few hours later on the red carpet, well it's blue really. Scarlett walks about and she is taking all the limelight from the stars of the film. Scarlett was born red, hence the name but as she has got older she became more light ginger-blonde.

All of a sudden a car pulls up and all the film crew and cameramen fix their lenses on Emma Thompson as she gets out of the car and walks towards us. I have always been a big fan of Emma Thompson ever since I saw her in that film 'Much Ado about Nothing'. I loved that film. There are flashes of camera bulbs everywhere, the noise is deafening. Scarlett is just sitting looking around at everyone, I'm sure she thinks everyone is here to see her. As Emma Thompson gets nearer, I look at Alex who is wearing a beautiful dress which is sparkling in the lights. I smile at her and we both take a deep breath.

As Emma gets nearer she smiles and her dress looks amazing. "Hello, you look lovely," Emma says to Alex. "Are you both enjoying yourselves?"

"Yes, we are thank you," Alex says.

"Lovely dress," I say.

"Thank you, who is this?" Emma says pointing downwards.

"This is Scarlett," I reply. Emma crouches down and starts to stroke her. I hand Emma the lead and they both walk towards the main door of the theatre where all the press are waiting. Emma stands there for about 15 minutes with Scarlett, while the press take lots of photos. They both seem to be enjoying themselves. After the press has finished taking the photos, we follow Emma into the theatre to watch the film. Scarlett decides to have a wee before going in, well better outside on the carpet than in the theatre. As we walk in, there are people everywhere; we grab some popcorn and walk to our seats. As Alex and I settle down, I watch Scarlett as she lies down and goes to sleep without a care in the world. I sit there and think about the past two years and chuckle.

Why are we at the premier of Nanny McPhee and the Big Bang with a woolly pig? Let me take you back to when we bought a small-holding in Shropshire and all will become clear.

***

I was sitting at home one spring morning drinking a coffee after dropping Alex off at school. The sun was streaming through our lounge window bouncing off a scenic country picture hanging in the far corner. I sat there looking at the picture with my coffee in hand whilst a smile came over my face. I had a feeling that I was about to do something stupid; nothing new there.

Leaving the house feeling the sun on my back and with a skip in my step I walked down the high street. We lived in the centre of Shrewsbury, a lovely three story house that used to be where Charles Darwin went to school. Strolling through the town, I was looking at all the different and unusual shops Shrewsbury has. Coming up was the estate agent area of Shrewsbury; I spied out of the corner of my eye a property in the window. Walking up to the window there in front of me was a detached country house looking very sad. The house pulled me into the agent's and half an hour later I had booked for Alex and I to see the house at the end of the day.

It was time to collect Alex from school. "Hi Alex, how was your day?" I asked.

"Good Dad, same as always. I am in three races on sports day."

Alex was a good runner. "That's great, I'm looking forward to the day." Going to Alex's sports day, we always ended up having the rest of the children around us, as I would take enough to feed all of Shrewsbury. There was never any food left.

"Come on Alex, we are going to see a house," I said.

"What for?"

"To possibly move to."

"Really? Wow, where is it?"

"I don't know."

Alex started to laugh. "Yep, that's my dad," she said.

"It's a new adventure," I replied. "Let's see where it takes us."

I had pulled off the main road and found myself travelling along a narrow farm road. I knew this as there was muck all over the place, even up the hedges.

"Wow, that's a lot of muck," Alex said. My white car was turning grey very quickly. Dirt was flying everywhere. "Mmmm, I had better slow down," I thought, plus my car had already slid sideways nearly ending up in the ditch.

Driving up to an even narrower road (well, a dirt track) I was thinking I might get my car stuck driving along it. In for a penny in for a pound I thought.

"You ready, Alex?"

"Yes," came the excited reply. Setting off down the track I was driving a lot slower than before, and there were fields everywhere.

Turning the corner I skidded to a halt. Climbing out of the car with my mouth open wide, Alex stepped out too. I turned to look at her; she had a smile a mile wide.

"Let's leave the car here and walk down Dad."

"Ok, Alex." As we walked towards the house I had a feeling come over me as if I was coming home. Holding Alex's hand tightly, we walked towards the man standing by the door who would show us around. After looking around the house, which I noted needed gutting, Alex had already picked her room, where her bed was going and what colour the room would be. I was looking at what walls to knock out! I'd better get someone else to do that with my track record, I thought.

As we came out of the house I asked how big the garden was. John, the agent said all the land either side of the house was part of the sale.

"Steve," he said, "look ahead of you. All the land in front as far as you can see to the woods. It's sixty acres in all."

"No way, you're kidding," I said.

Alex looked at me. "What are we going to do with all of that, Dad?"

I giggled, grabbed her hand and walked back to the car. As we walked off I turned back to John saying, "Yes we will take it, see you in the morning."

Alex grabbed my hand tightly, smiling at me. "Oh golly, oh golly," she said running off towards the car shouting. "We've bought a farm!!"

I turned to look back at the farm and fields around it, not knowing what lay ahead or how it would change our lives. But it certainly did, and for the better.

CHAPTER 2
THE WORK STARTS HERE

We had bought a small-holding on the edge of Shrewsbury about seven miles out of the town. Before we could move in, the farmhouse needed to be completely refurbished as it was derelict. I was excited about the project and could not wait to get stuck into the work that needed doing, but I was a little apprehensive about what needed to be done and my role.

Let me just put you in the picture what I am like. Well, I have never used a drill in my life, I own one but it's never been out of its box, unless my mother comes over to put some curtain poles up for me. When she did, I watched her using some brown plastic things and pushing them into the hole she had just drilled. "What are those?" I asked. My mother sighed. "They're rawlplugs, son, you put the screws into them to hold them secure." "Oh!" I said. I have tried to put shelves up in the past and the next day they are not on the wall, but on the floor. I put a picture up over my bed once and was woken up in the middle of the night by it falling off the wall and breaking my nose. God that so hurt.

When it comes to DIY I am good at knocking things down or pulling stuff out, well thinking about it I have had my moments with that as well. I also have times when I do not think something through thoroughly before I act on it. Ideas pop into my head which I think are right and plausible. Take for instance the time I bought a greenhouse. I do not like to admit to this, I sound such a wally, but here goes.

Well, this was a few years ago when I was much younger, I was twenty-one to be precise. After buying the greenhouse, I had seen and heard on the news something about the problem with the atmosphere, the ozone layer and global warming. I had heard it was to do with the greenhouse effect. I know, before you start shaking your heads. I put two and two together and came up with God knows what. Yes! I did think it was to do with too many greenhouses being put up in people's gardens. I thought the plants gave off carbon monoxide and when in a greenhouse it intensifies the amount given off. Well that is what I had worked out in my head. I thought I would do my bit for the planet, so I did not build it. The greenhouse sat in my garden for a few months stacked against the wall of the house. One sunny afternoon I had some friends round for a barbeque and they asked about my greenhouse and why I had not put it up. When I told them about the greenhouse effect, they all rolled around laughing, in tears. "You plonker Steve, it's not to do with greenhouses in gardens, it's to do with pollution from cars and factories and the like and it causes holes in the atmosphere." All of a sudden, realisation came over me. I felt a right Charlie; I even found myself a few days later buying a telescope so I could look to see if I could see the holes. While I was in the garden looking up into the sky through the telescope, I thought to myself. "What a tit I am." After that I really did feel like a plonker. I know I'm special and yes I still have the telescope to this day… Well, getting back to the farm and what happened there.

I arrived at the farm after dropping Alex off at school; where to start was the first thing that came to mind. As I walked around the house, I was taking note of what needed doing. All the wooden floors and ceilings needed replacing, the floors, where tiles needed digging up and replacing as they had sunk and there was no damp course. The walls needed plastering and all the wiring was shot, there was no central heating, the bathroom and kitchen needed replacing as it looked like it was over 400 years old and the cellar was under four feet of water. The house was a complete mess.

"Where do I start," I said to myself. I walked upstairs and picked the far corner of the master bedroom, grabbed a large hammer and went for it. I started knocking the ceiling down. I did not think about the amount of black dust-like stuff that would be up there. As I was pulling the ceiling down, I was getting more and more covered; luckily I had thought of wearing goggles and a face mask, see I'm not completely useless. I arrived at the farm at about 9.30 am and all of a sudden it was 3 pm, where had the time gone? Now I had to get Alex. I arrived at the school to get her and was met with a lot of looks from the other parents.

Alex said, "What on earth have you been doing, Dad, you're filthy?"

I looked in the wing mirror of the car; the only white bits on my face were where I had been wearing my goggles and face mask. We both started to laugh. We headed back to the farm with fish and chips in hand. Alex wanted to get stuck in too. We were there until 8 p.m. where we both went at it knocking ceilings out all over the house and the black dust was flying around everywhere. We were laughing so much we looked like two chimney sweeps. Before long the place was getting stripped back to its bare brick and original timbers. I had decided on a local guy and his two sons to do all the work on the house. His name was Derrick and his two sons Toby and Freddy, they were in their twenties, while Derrick was about sixty years old. He worked like he was a forty-year-old. They were all amazing and worked so hard.

I remember one afternoon I was working in the large inglenook fireplace I had found and was in the middle of knocking all the brick work out when I heard a shout. "Steve, stop!" Derrick shouted, as he ran towards me pushing me out of the way. Apparently, I had knocked all the supports out for the chimney and it was about to fall in on the house.

"Well, how was I supposed to know that?" I said.

"Toby! Freddy! Quick! Bring in the supports," Derrick shouted.

"What's wrong?" I said.

"Out of the way Steve," Derrick said, shaking his head at me. "The chimney is about to fall in."

"Oh!" I said.

Freddy was crying with laughter. "You are a plonker, Steve." We all started to laugh, except Derrick. He did not see the funny side until the supports were in place. Then I piped up, "Is this a bad time to tell you about the wall I have knocked out upstairs?"

"What?" they said in unison as they all ran upstairs from all directions (there were two staircases). "Oh! Christ," I heard. "Get a lintel quick, Toby! We need to put this in before the ceiling comes down."

"Shall I make a cuppa?" I shouted.

"Do you think you can, without doing any damage in the kitchen?"

"Ha ha, you are funny," I said.

Derrick came downstairs and demanded, "Don't you dare try to knock anything else out."

"Shall I go outside and burn the rubbish that has come out of the house?" I said, as I handed over the cuppas to Derrick and his sons.

"Good idea," said Derrick, "you can't do anything wrong out there."

I went outside to build the bonfire and burn all the timbers and other rubbish that had been pulled out of the house. There was so much to burn. Derrick and his sons got on with fixing all the damage I had done. I still think it wasn't my fault. Anyone could have made the same mistake!

"Ok, hmmm, where shall I build this fire?" I thought. Suddenly I had an idea; on one side of the house two large oak trees stood. They were only about six feet away from the house but that did not enter my head. Anyway, I knew they would have to come down. We had permission from the local council to bring them down as they were too close to the house. They were taller than the house and I had a quote from a Tree Surgeon. He wanted seven hundred pounds, which I thought was daylight robbery. I saw a way of saving money, this is where my idea came from and wow, what an idea it was.

"I know," I thought, "I will implode the two trees!" I had seen buildings on TV being imploded and they came straight down. I could not see why I couldn't do this with the trees. So I would build the bonfire at the bottom of the trees and set it on fire, this would also burn the trees down. I knew building a fire alone around the trees would not work. I needed gun powder and I would blow them up.

I got started with old timbers and floor boards; to be honest, I went looking for anything that could burn and before long I had built a large bonfire between the two trees and all around them, it looked pretty good it was about ten feet high. "For these two trees to come down this fire needs to be big," I thought, so I also poured about fifty litres of diesel and thirty litres of petrol over it. I also got about ten bales of straw to get it going from an old barn on the farm.

Now this is where my plan really came together. It was getting close to Guy Fawkes' Night and I had some fireworks in the car, well when I say fireworks, the boot was full with about ten large boxes of display fireworks, about three hundred in all. I love bonfire night. I should have been Guy Fawkes as this is where the gun powder idea came from. I had also heard about putting coffee and washing powder in it, so it would make a bigger explosion. I don't know where I had heard that from, anyway I went into the house looking for them. Toby saw me walking out of the house with a jar of coffee and a box of washing powder. He just shook his head and walked off.

As the two trees were hollow on the inside and shaped like cannon holes, I thought, if I cut open the fireworks and pour the gun powder along with the coffee and washing powder into the hollows of the trees and stuff some big ones in and pack it down with hay as you do with a real cannon and then pack it down with wadding, I think that's what they call it. Then I thought if I put large boulders on top and other large items which I compacted down and throw a load more fireworks on top for good measure, "This will bring them down." The petrol and diesel was poured all over the bonfire and I poured loads inside each trunk, about twenty litres in each. I went back into the house. "Have you got a lighter

Derrick?"

"Yeah, here you go Steve, all ok out there?" he asked.

"No problem Derrick, trust me," I said. I could hear Toby and Freddy laughing upstairs.

"Sod off," I said as I walked back outside. I was looking at the mound of stuff I had built around the trees. "Wow! What a good job I have done, all on my own without the help of anyone else." I thought, with a smile on my face. I had even thought about leaving a trail of petrol from the fire, back to me so, not to get hurt when it went up.

"This is really going to work." I thought. Well, out with a match, I started to light the trail of petrol, not realising I had spilt quite a lot on my wellies. Wow! The fire went up really well but so did my wellies.

"Oh, Christ," I shouted as I tried to get my wellies off. I turned around and ran to where there was a tub of water, with my wellies ablaze. I jumped into the barrel and pulled them off. "Phew!" No burns, just wrecked the boots and wet socks and trousers, so no real harm done. As I turned 'round there was a large thunderous bang. "Wow!" I thought. One of the boulders flew out of the tree, cleared the house and landed on next door's shed. The fire was blazing out of control, the two trees were on fire and it was setting the roof of the farmhouse on fire.

"Hmmm I did not think of this," I thought. The fireworks were shooting everywhere. "Wow! What do I do now," I thought.

Derrick and his sons came running out of the house when they heard the bang, to see fireworks coming out of the tree. Then there was an almighty second boom as another large object shot out of the tree like a cannon ball. "Wow!" I shouted. "Look at that one go." It shot clean over the house. I was trying not to look impressed with myself. Derrick was running around and shouting.

"It's like a war zone, what have you done Steve, what have you done?" He then got on the phone to ring the fire brigade, while his two sons rolled on the ground laughing and taking photos of the fire on their phones to send to their friends.

Freddy was videoing what was happening. "I'm going to put this on YouTube. Bloody hell, Steve what are you like?"

"I thought it would bring the trees down," I said. "I was trying to implode them like you do a building," I said.

"Ha! They are trees, not buildings," Toby said.

"Well, I think I may have needed a bit more gun powder."

"What was that?" Derrick said.

"Oh nothing, Derrick." Thinking, "I had better keep quiet now."

When the fire brigade arrived, they could not believe what they saw and started to take pictures with their own phones. "We could see the fire from over a mile away," they said, laughing,

"Don't look at me," said Derrick. "It's that plonker's fault over there." They started to get all their kit together to put the fire out. They had to be careful as they had to dodge the odd firework or two. Then a third loud bang and another two boulders flew out, one just missing the fire engine.

"Christ!" they shouted. "What's inside them?"

"Just a bit of gun powder and some petrol," I replied. I was not going to tell them how much. By now the trees were fully ablaze, and so was half of the roof on the house, crikey! It took them several hours to put out the fire. The flames must have been twenty metres high. I must admit I was proud of it but kept that to myself.

When the fire was finally out I was told the trees were a danger and I had to get the Tree Surgeon in to bring them down. They would not leave until he came out so I had to get him there on an emergency call-out basis. When they had all left, I had to pay the tree man more for coming out on an emergency. It cost me a whopping eight hundred and fifty pounds and the fire brigade bill was a further five hundred pounds. All in all, an expensive day. As Derrick left, he was just shaking his head laughing.

"Derrick I am not here tomorrow," I shouted.

"Thank God for that," he replied.

After the trees had been taken down, we had the problem of the roots to pull out. While Derrick and his sons were busy working inside the house, I got onto a local digger hire company. About two hours later they turned up with the digger; they unloaded it and left.

"How difficult can it be to drive one of these?" I thought. I went up to the house and shouted to Derrick, "I have a digger here, how hard is it to work?"

At that, one of his sons ran down the stairs and said, "Don't touch it." He came outside and started it up. I also had a dumper delivered and he showed me how to use it and I had no problem driving it. So now I was involved in the dumping of all the soil which I enjoyed. Driving the dumper up and down the fields was great fun and the weather was really hot so it was a great time for doing this type of work. I only crashed it twice and we will not talk about the day I thought I could drive the digger and drove it into a pond. It was not that big of a deal, we pulled it out the next day with a tractor!

About six months later all the work was about complete. The house was finished, new kitchens and bathrooms, new oil central heating, log burners had been fitted in the lounge, kitchen and dining room. The house had been completely decorated and looked great. Outside, the septic tank had been put in and so had all the new roads. The garden had been landscaped with ponds and a large vegetable patch.

There was a large area off the garden that spread off to three sides of the house with a large patio to the front of the house. Alex had been coming down every evening after school to help out and I had not created any more problems for Derrick and his sons. I had been helping outside, which is where they preferred to keep me. Alex had been on the dumper with me and loved sitting in the bucket. The day had come to move in; we were so excited. The removal van came on time; we started early in the morning and were all moved in by late afternoon. We moved on a Saturday and by Sunday evening the house was practically all finished and everything was in its place. Alex had eventually decided where she wanted everything in her room. We had only moved her bed five times! Now the bedroom looked great and Alex had made the most of the room and had laid it out better than I could have.

We were sitting on the patio on Sunday evening talking and enjoying the spring weather. It was now April and the weather had warmed up earlier than normal. As we were sitting there eating, Alex said, "Dad when are we going to start getting the animals?"

"You know, I had completely forgotten about the animals; where do we start? We also need to get planting the vegetable patch, what are we going to plant, Alex?"

"How about strawberries?" she replied.

"I thought you would say that," knowing that was Alex's favourite.

"Can we also get a dog, Dad?" she said.

"What made you think of that then?" I said.

"Well, Alex said, "we have the space now and I would do all the walking."

"Yeah I bet," I thought. After Alex had gone to bed I started to make all the plans for the vegetable patch and what animals to have first. "Where do I get them from?" I thought. I went to bed feeling very contented with life and could not wait to see what lay ahead. If we only knew what path this would take us on.

CHAPTER 3
FARM LOOKING GOOOD!

Still thinking where I was going to start, I took Alex to school. Alex said, "Dad?"

"Yes Alex?" I replied.

"When are we going to have a house-warming party?"

"Mmmm party, not thought of that, what a great idea," was my reply. I love any excuse to have a party and I could get some fireworks too. "Great, good idea, I'll start the plans to arrange it."

When I got back, I made a note of all the friends to ask and Alex's friends and parents. Wow! The list was at two hundred and fifty. "Can't fit them all into the house," I thought. "I know, I'll get a couple of cheap marquees. We need music, I wonder if Freddy will do it as I know he has been a DJ at other gigs and brings all his own kit."

I looked on the 'net for an act for the evening as well. I found a band that looked good and they would do two, one hour stints and the DJ would play his stuff in between. This was coming together well; I had also hired a temporary loo for outside and arranged to rig up a load of outside lights. A friend of mine was coming to cook a pig outside, so everyone could have pork baps and I had bought loads and loads of fireworks.

It was the morning before the party and everything was going well; friends had come 'round to help put up the marquees, as they all knew how much help I would be. I was told to stay away. Everyone was busy except me. What could I do? For some reason it just came to me, "I know! I'll sweep the chimney."

The room to the front of the house had an open fireplace and it had never been used as it was blocked. I knew in the shed there was a complete set of chimney-sweep brushes with extensions my mother had given me. "How hard can it be?" I thought. I had seen Mary Poppins. It did not look hard when he did it. So without saying anything to anyone, I thought it would be a surprise to get it cleared and have a nice roaring fire as the other fireplaces had log burners in them. The house looked great so I had to be careful. I started to push the large brush head up the huge fireplace. I looked up, there did not seem to be too much there blocking it, so I would not need a sheet over it, just one on the floor at the base. I started to connect the rods together and pushed up then added another connection. I had fixed about seven connections when it came to a stop. All I had to do was give it a real good push and the stuff blocking the chimney would come out at the top and keep the room clean just like in Mary Poppins. I heard the squeak of a door from behind me.

"Dad what are you doing?" Alex asked.

"Nothing, I am just cleaning the chimney." I gave it an almighty push and at that, there was a roar coming down the chimney. I looked up and as I did so, a great big cloud of soot came down and out. Alex screamed and started laughing. At that, other people ran into the room.

"Oh my God Steve, what have you done?" I pulled my head from out of the chimney, my face was black and so was the rest of me, and Alex was covered in soot. The cream carpet and walls were no longer cream but a grey sooty colour. "Oh knickers, why do these things always happen to me?" I said.

Everyone started laughing. "Come on, where's the hoover? Let's start cleaning." After all that, the chimney was still blocked, I could not believe it.

A few hours later, everything was ready. The loo and lights had arrived. The house was now clean and tidy. The pig was cooked and cut ready to go in baps with apple sauce and stuffing. The DJ and band had arrived and were all set up in the marquee. Everything was going to plan, which considering my past record, was an achievement. About two hundred friends turned up and a lot of Alex's friends were there to. We all had a great night. It was time to light the fireworks. All my friends had insisted I set them up a field away and I had two helpers whom I think had wished they had not offered. As we lit some of the big ones, they fell over and shot off across the field setting off other fireworks as they went, just missing one of my friends, who happened to be helping. A display that was supposed to last about forty minutes was over in about half the time, due to the fireworks going off and setting the other ones off. I had set them up too close to each other. I really made a bit of a mess of it. It was lucky we were wearing gloves and goggles as we would have had burns. One went off close to my face but thankfully, I was ok.

"From now on I will only go to organised displays," I said, as we let off the last ones. Both my friends laughed and agreed. We left the fields and walked back to the house laughing all the way and they were happy they were still alive. They could not believe I was able to get commercial fireworks. It seemed like a good idea at the time. The party went well and we all danced the night away. All the food was eaten and the weather was really warm. The last person left at about 2 am and we had cleared everything away by 3 am. All in all, a great night.

Next morning, I went into Alex's bedroom early, with a surprise which my neighbour had been looking after for me. I walked into her room and plonked onto her bed a liver-spot Dalmatian puppy. It started to lick her face. I left her screaming in her room.

"Oh my God, oh my God," was all I could hear from her as I walked down the stairs. As I got to the bottom of the stairs, I got my black bundle from the lounge. I had bought a black female Labrador puppy, which I had decided to call Cerys. Alex had called her dog Ruby and they both got on well together. When I watched Alex playing with the puppies, I cannot remember seeing her so happy. Alex had taken it on herself to train both of them, which she was doing well. Before long they were both house trained and followed her everywhere. The puppies were so well behaved, never going upstairs and never chewing the furniture.

It was now late morning and I heard a knock on the door.

The first delivery of the day was the chicken house I had bought online. It could hold about twenty hens in it and came on wheels. The delivery chap helped me to site it at the top of the garden. Then all the fencing poles with wire fencing arrived, along with barbed wire, nails and loads of other fencing materials. I was planning on building all the fencing around the hens myself, which was going to take the best part of the weekend. While I was doing the fencing I had Alex running around the garden with the new puppies. They spent most of the time together on the trampoline. I never knew at that point how much time I would be spending on the trampoline.

I was surprised with myself and so was Alex...by Sunday evening all the fencing was finished. I had help from a local farmer who had come to put the six foot gates on but everything else I had done myself. Not looking as good as it should, the fencing was loose, as I did not tighten it properly. My farmer friend went over it with a special tool, not sure what you would call it but it was a big long thing and made a better job of it. Well I did try. I sat there with a cup of tea in my hands, looking at what I had achieved, it looked really good.

The following Saturday was the smallholders' show at Builth Wells, which is where I was hoping to buy the chickens and learn more about running a small farm.

Saturday came quicker than we thought. We settled Cerys and Ruby at Alex's friend's house for the day, agreeing to leave early as it would take two hours, at least, to get there. We arrived at about 10 am and parked up. There was loads to see. The first building we went into had ducks, chickens, geese and all other types of birds, some I had never heard of. We looked around and ended up buying some Warrens, Reds, some sort of grey hens with spots on them. They looked good. Anyway, in all we bought fourteen chickens and said we would pick them up at the end of the day. We paid the cost on average, seven pounds per chicken, so not bad and they were about two weeks away from laying eggs. We moved off to the rest of the show. Around the next corner we came across some llamas which Alex really liked.

"Can we have some, Dad?"

"What are we going to do with them, Alex?"

"They look good, Dad." I was told by the owner that they keep the foxes away, so good to know as we were having chickens. I wondered if the guy selling chickens had a deal going with the woman who was selling the llamas or were they husband and wife, mmm. I don't know how it happened but I walked away after buying three llamas which were mother, daughter and son. They were going to deliver them on Sunday evening after the show had finished. They cost me seven hundred and fifty pounds which I thought was not bad but what was I going to do with them? God only knew. We spent the rest of the show looking at all sorts of animals, even ferrets. We had not been anywhere near the pig area all day and they were now doing the judging of the different types, so we wandered over. As we got there, we could not believe all the different types of pigs. We watched how they moved them around the ring with a square white board. I do not know what it was about them, but I found I really liked them and they made me smile.

They had set up a course for the pigs to go over. It was so funny, the pigs did not want to do what they were told and they were running around everywhere, with their owners chasing after them. When I asked if there were any for sale, I found out the ones which were for sale had been all sold. "Oh bugger!" I thought. "Never mind, it's not meant to be," I said. As we left the show, I had a big smile on my face.

"You really loved that Dad, didn't you?" said Alex.

"You're right I did, just a shame we could not buy any pigs."

"Dad!" shouted Alex, "the chickens!" We had forgotten

them. "Oh, Dad what are you like," she said. We turned the car around and were just in time to get them, phew.

"We were just about to leave," said the owners.

"I'm so sorry," I said. I got their card, so if I needed any more hens I had a contact. On arrival at home it was getting late; we unloaded the chickens and settled them down for the night in their new home. I was surprised to see them all just take themselves off to bed without me having to chase them into their house. "That was easy," I thought. All I needed to do was go inside and settle down with a nice cup of tea, and relax while thinking about what had happened that day. A big smile came over my face as I fell asleep in the chair, contented.

The next morning I went outside with a cup of tea to watch the hens. As I opened their door on the hens' house they all rushed out and started digging around. They were fascinating to watch. "Wow!" As I looked in I found our first two eggs. "No way!" I thought. "They are early starters." After feeding them and making sure they had water I went back inside to make boiled eggs for Alex and me. When Alex went outside with Ruby and Cerys, I followed and watched what went on. Alex was on the trampoline, the puppies were running around barking at the chickens, while they just strutted around scratching at the ground ignoring the dogs. I had started to dig the vegetable patch, ready for the planting of the spuds and carrots and I had already planted the strawberries. Later that day came the arrival of the llamas. We unloaded them into the field opposite the house so we could keep an eye on them. With the help of a friend we built a temporary shelter for them which ended up being better than we thought. It was good enough for them to live in. Everything was starting to come together. I sat talking to a friend with a cuppa in hand, looking across the fields watching the llamas with the sun setting behind them, we both agreed it was a beautiful setting.

Later that evening, I was reading the local newspaper and saw an advert for some piglets. I phoned straight away and was told they had ten piglets left. After a long conversation about the pigs, which were Saddlebacks, they're a white pig with a black saddle across its back, a black face and trotters, if you were wondering. I arranged to have a look at them on Friday before picking Alex up from school. Friday came quickly and finding the farm took me longer than I thought. The pigs looked great and he had told me he was selling up and needed to get rid of the pigs. Before I knew what I was doing, I asked what he wanted for all ten pigs. He told me three hundred and fifty pounds. I offered him two hundred and fifty pounds and he said, "If you take them now, it's a deal."

I looked at my car. "Oh! Ok," I said, "done." I drove a Volvo estate. "Oh dear, mmm." The next thing I knew, I had folded the seats down and we were lifting the pigs into the back of my car. One by one they went in and sure enough, one by one they started to pee and poo in the back of the car. I was starting to think that this was not such a good idea after all. I paid the man and set off to get Alex from school with all ten pigs in the back of my car. Wow! They started to throw up on the way, never smelt anything like it before. As I turned up to get Alex she just looked at me, the car and the pigs and shaking her head as she got into the car said, "Dad what are you doing?"

"Well…" I started to say.

"Just get us home so I can get away from this smell and we can get them out," she said. We had all the windows down on the way home and Alex had her head out all the way. I must admit the smell was so bad and the noise was terrible. Their loud squealing noise went right through your head.

When we got home we unloaded the pigs into the back garden. "Dad, where are we going to put them tonight?"

"Oh, I had not thought of that Alex, they will need some

cover." We went into the house for a cup of tea and to think about it. While Alex was upstairs I had an idea. I started to empty the furniture out of the kitchen. An hour later the kitchen was empty of all furniture.

I went outside to see the pigs. "Oh my God." They had destroyed the lawn. How did they dig all of that up in just an hour? There were large holes everywhere. I quickly rounded them up and brought them into the kitchen with food. That is how I found out that pigs will do anything for food. I left them in the kitchen with a bale of straw for them to sleep on and water and went into the lounge to settle down.

Alex came downstairs, "Dad you haven't done what I think you have?" she said.

"What?" I replied.

"Put the pigs in the kitchen?"

"Yes why?" I said. Alex just shook her head and went back upstairs laughing. I could hear her saying, "Oh Dad." When I went to bed that evening there was not a noise to be heard coming from the kitchen. All was well I thought.

It was about 3 am when the noise started. I went into the kitchen, "Oh my God!" I said. What a mess and the smell, there was poo everywhere and I never knew a pig could pee so much. There was gallons of it, all over the floor. They had managed to dig up the quarry tiling floor, pull all of the kitchen unit doors off and had eaten loads of food. Wow! What a mess. I opened the back door and they all ran out. After getting Alex to school, I came home and got the jet wash set up and started to jet wash the kitchen. I had to get a specialist firm in to clean the kitchen and builders in to replace the floor and kitchen units.

I phoned the local farmer from up the road and his two sons came down to help me. When Dan and Ken arrived they came into the kitchen to see me jet washing it. "You never kept the pigs in here last night?" they said laughing.

"Well it seemed a good idea at the time," I told them.

"You're not right, Steve," they said in unison as they left the kitchen, shaking their heads, laughing.

By the end of the day I had the garden fencing redone, as they had said the fencing I had put up would not keep them in and they would rip it up. Also, as they leaned on some of it, it had fallen down. "I only put that up last week," I told them, laughing.

"Leave all the fencing to us from now on," they told me.

"Oh! Ok," I said feeling pretty useless. While they were building the fencing, I built the pigs a shelter from some galvanized sheeting. I had been watching a programme on the BBC about Victorian farming and had seen them put a Victorian floor into their pig house. I did the same with mine. I laid a peat cover on the floor about 4 inches deep and pushed empty glass bottles into the peat which covered it fully. Then I made a cement mix and covered all the bottles, so you could not see them. This would make the floor cool in the summer and warm in the winter. It looked great when finished and I was surprised with myself and so was everyone else.

When finished, the pig house looked great and the two lads had done a great job of the fencing. "Just the lawn to put right, along with the kitchen," they said.

"Oh sod off!" I said to them laughing. The kitchen smelt horrible for four months, even after the specialist firm and builders had been in. To get the lawn looking right, it took another six months. The kitchen still had that horrible smell which just would not go, so I decided the only way to get rid of the smell was to get the commercial cleaners back in and spray it again, which did the job and the smell was finally gone.

The immediate problem I had was to find out how to look after the pigs which I had no idea about. That evening I looked on the internet and found a pig training course down south which was held every weekend. It was called Pig

Paradise and was run by a couple called Tony York and Carron McCann. I phoned them up they sounded really nice and they could not believe I had bought ten pigs before learning about how to look after them. They booked me a place on the following weekend as I needed their help quickly.

After trawling the internet, I booked a hotel for the night before. The course looked great. It was held on Saturday morning and started at 9 am. They had all types of pigs; they were all rare breeds and were all handled, so we were going to be able to get in with them and hold the piglets. "Wow! What fun," I thought as I read up on what else would happen that day. I was so excited. Alex and the puppies were going to stay with a school friend for the weekend. I would pick her up from school with the puppies and drop them off at her friend's, so all was well there. I had arranged for a neighbour to come 'round and feed the chickens and pigs over the weekend. They also would hang some hay out for the llamas and give them some apples so all was covered at home. I could not wait to go and was getting more and more excited. "Roll on the weekend," I thought.

CHAPTER 4
LIFE-CHANGING EVENT

I dropped Alex off at her friend's with Ruby and Cerys. I
then headed off with an overnight bag packed. I drove down
the M5 heading south staying near to Salisbury Plains. The
road was not bad and I made good time, the journey took
about four hours. The hotel I was staying at was in a place
called Warminster, a really nice place. Checking in went
smoothly, the room was not too small, with a really
comfortable double bed. I jumped into the shower and went
down to dinner. I was so hungry. The bar was at the back of
the hotel where they had a large list of traditional beers to try,
"Cool," I thought, looking for something new to try. I
ordered a pint and went in for dinner. The food was great. I
finished with a great apple crumble and custard. It was
yummy and I was full now. I headed off to my room with

another bitter in hand and settled down for the rest of the evening.

I was up early the next morning. I had a full English breakfast then left for the course with an excitement in my belly that I had not felt in years. Last time I felt like this was when I had met a girl from Devon when I was nineteen, whom I had fallen in love with but never had the guts to tell her. That was the one and only time I had really been in love; anyway getting back to the course. I arrived about thirty minutes early and was met by a lovely man. He was larger than life and had a smile and warmth about him. He looked so contented with life. "Hi, my name is Tony," he said, "and you are?"

"Hi I'm Steve, I'm a bit early."

"Never mind, come on in and meet Carron and have a cuppa," he said.

"Sounds good to me, Tony." Wow! Carron had the same glow about her; what was it that was making them so happy? "Hi Carron, I'm Steve."

"Hi, you're the chap from Shropshire who has just bought some pigs, I read your email." "Yes, that's right, so I thought I should come and learn about how to look after them."

Tony looked at me and said, "You mean to say you have

bought some pigs and do not know how to look after them?"

"I know nothing about them, except that I have bought ten saddleback pigs, they eat, wee and poo a lot, that's about it."

They both laughed. "You really have gone about this the wrong way. You should have come here before you bought them."

"Yeah, I know that now." I started to tell them about my experience with the pigs in the kitchen. Tony was crying with laughter.

"By the end of this weekend you will know all you will need to know for now and pick the rest up as you go. I have a great book you can take back with you." He was right, I used it like my bible for the pigs. It helped so much and could not have done pig rearing without it. If I needed Tony, he was always at the end of the phone and willing to help where he could. They were a great couple to have in your corner.

There were about twenty-two people on the course. Some had been bought 'the day out' as a birthday present. Others were thinking about buying some pigs, some were there just to learn about pigs. Last of all there was me, who had bought ten pigs and knew nothing about how to look after them, yep that was me!

The morning was spent getting to know a bit about the pigs and why we were all there. We learnt about why Tony and Carron were doing what they were doing. They bounced off each other and he was so funny. The course had started at 9 am, it was now 11 am and we were heading out to meet the pigs. We all got changed and put on our boots and overalls. I was very excited as we walked up the hill with Tony and the rest of the group. Carron stayed behind as she was preparing a great roast lunch for us, pork of course.

As we arrived at the open pig pens, they all started to run out of their houses. There were pigs everywhere and the piglets were allowed to roam anywhere, the whole place looked great. I was surprised as there was no horrible smell, just a pleasant piggy smell. Hard to describe - kind of peppery smell, but very sweet, a bit like how a new born puppy smells. All the pigs were hand reared and we were allowed to get in with them. As I climbed into the first pen, the pigs came up to me and just started rubbing against me. Before long I was on the floor lying next to them giving the pigs belly rubs. Did you know pigs love to have their bellies rubbed? You just start scratching their sides and they roll over onto their back to have their belly rubbed and they will stay like that for hours as long as you rub them. While I was there, I started to realise what it was that was making Tony and Carron so happy, it was the pigs and their way of life.

We were shown how to inject them, how much food they eat, how to tell when they are ill, what size of pigs go with which house...we learnt so much. I also found out that you can give pigs fresh fruit as long as it has not been through your kitchen. Pigs cannot eat oranges or anything acidic, as this will give them stomach ulcers and if they eat parsnips, this will give them mouth ulcers.

There are very strict rules on looking after pigs if you are intending on selling the meat to the public. The one amazing thing is that everything in the pig world happens in threes; they come into season every three weeks, it lasts for three days, when they are in pig (pregnant), the piglets are born in three months, three weeks and three days and three glasses of wine later...weird I know. You feed pigs twice a day, three pounds of food in the morning and three pounds of food in the afternoon. Pigs always eat. So if they are not eating their food, you know they are ill. As long as they have water, food and shelter they will be fine. When they are ill you either inject them with penicillin or an anti-inflammatory and you give them one injection a day over a three day period. Did you know you only get bacon from a girl pig? Boy pigs can only be used for pork or sausage. When a boy pig is older than forty weeks, the meat can taint which makes it inedible. After a while I started to realise that there was not a lot into looking after pigs and knowing my track record that's a good thing. I fell in love with them and wanted to know more and more about them. The breeds they had at the farm were: Gloucestershire old spot, Large Black, Berkshires, Saddleback, Tamworth, Middle Whites, Kune-Kune, British Lop, Oxford Sandy & Black and my favourite and theirs were the Mangalitza.

The Mangalitza is a funny looking pig, it looks like a sheep. It has a woolly coat like a sheep but it's a pig. I called it a Shig. They come in three colours blonde, red and swallow belly which is a black pig with a white belly.

We found out that a nose ring is fitted to a pig to stop it rutting the soil up. When a pig lives outside, it gets all its vitamins from eating the soil and the odd worm. Pigs will eat nearly everything and they could eat a whole human body in a week, leaving nothing. Their teeth are so strong that they can bite clean through an avocado stone. They need a good house to live in which is called a pig ark, either made from wood, plastic or tin…or almost anything. But they can cost a lot, anything from three hundred pounds, second-hand up to six hundred pounds. Straw bedding is what they like to sleep on and they should be kept out of the wind. They do like their comfort, which I was to find out more and more.

Pigs will very rarely mess in their beds and are very clean animals. A lot of the sayings do mean something, like 'pigs can fly'. Well, they can. What I mean is, when a mother pig is eating and her piglets are trying to push their way into eat her food she will flick them into the air with her nose and mummy pig can sometimes flick her piglets six feet into the air, that's where the saying 'pigs can fly' comes from. You also have to make sure that you keep your pigs wormed on a regular basis making sure that no worms can be passed onto the piglets. There was quite a bit to learn but nothing too difficult. They also had a book you could buy at the end of the course which I would say is the bible on keeping pigs. It tells you everything you need to know.

When we went back inside I found myself asking Carron what was for lunch. "Roast pork," she said, shaking her head. "What did you think we were going to cook?" We all sat down for an amazing roast pork dinner. Wow! Best roast I had ever had, the flavours were amazing. I sat there with a smile a mile wide on my face, I was so happy.

At the end of the day I was buzzing and could not think of anything else. I thanked them both and left for home. It was supposed to be a four hour journey home but I had a slight problem! I left Salisbury and headed for the M4 motorway.

Then I approached the M5 motorway and my excuse for this was being deep in thought about the day's events. I turned left onto the M5 motorway when I should have gone right. After about an hour I came across a sign saying Taunton. All I could think was, "Mmm, that's where I had that great weekend with Four Crosses Young Farmers on a weekend exchange." I joined Young Farmers when I was 18. Living in the countryside you can join this organisation. Young Farmers is a way for young boys and girls to meet to arrange events like balls, sports events, drama competitions and many more social activities. This is a large organisation which is spread across the UK where they raise money for charities whilst having fun. After a few months of being a member I said to a friend Peter whilst in the Four Crosses pub after drinking our fourth pint, "Blimey, Peter there seems to be a lot of drinking involved being a member."

Peter said as he laughed, "Yeh, hard work this charity fundraising." I began to chuckle to myself thinking about all the fun we had back then. "Where have the years gone?" I thought.

I started to think there was something amiss when I noticed the motorway was coming to an end and there was a sign saying welcome to Exeter. Yep, I had gone the wrong way down the motorway! Instead of getting nearer to home, I had gone in the opposite direction.

"Oh knickers," I thought, "why does this always happen to me?" After stopping at a service garage and filling the car up, I turned around and seven hours later I arrived home.

CHAPTER 5
WHAT NEXT

The day's events just would not leave my head. It was all I could think about. The pigs! That's why Tony and Carron were both so happy. They had been so helpful on the course they had told me I could call them at any time if I needed help. I had also arranged to buy two red Mangalitza piglets from them, which I would pick up in a couple of months.

When I got home it was very late. I went for a walk around the farm checking up on all the animals and making plans. I would be picking up Alex and the puppies the next day after school. I could not sleep that evening and by morning I had planned the lay-out of the whole field opposite the house. We were going to have eighteen pig pens built, with roads in-between so it would be easy to feed them and to move them from pen to pen. I could also give some of the pens a rest and to show people around when visiting. I had decided to have rare breed pigs and sell them for either meat or breeding stock to other farms. I had also decided that the pig farm was going to have people come and visit on pig days (Red Letter days). They would pay me to come and help clean out the pig pens and be able to sit with them and hold the piglets. They would also learn about them and later that afternoon they would finish the day off with sausage sandwiches.

But how was I going to build the pens? I knew I could get the houses, as I had already bought four wooden pig houses, when I was on the pig course and would have them in two weeks' time. "I know, I thought, I will ask Dan and Ken, I am sure they will be able to build the pens."

The next day I phoned Dan and he came straight over. I told him what I was planning to do. He said, "No problem." they would be able to do it and would use a tractor with a post banger on the front to bang the posts in.

I watched as they started two days later. "Wow!" I thought. Ken would hold the post and Dan would send a large metal hammer down onto it off the back of the tractor. "Blimey," I thought, "if he gets that wrong then Ken will either lose an arm or his head." I asked if I could have a go but for some reason Dan would not let me anywhere near the tractor. The pig houses arrived a couple of weeks later and Dan and Ken helped with building them. Well, to tell the truth they built them and I made the coffee. I did have the idea to put them off the ground on some telegraph poles which I had found up the field. Well not quite up the field, I saw them on the side of the road one day and asked Ken if he could pick them up in his trailer. Well, they had just been sitting there.

That evening Alex and I were watching a program called Victorian Farm on the BBC and they were talking about how people looked after pigs in those days. I sat up with excitement. It was confirming that what I was doing was the right way forward. "Alex," I said, "that's great…they kept them free range back then, and we are doing the same."

I always wanted to put the welfare of the pigs first, just like the Victorians did. I would do the floors like they did, having them roaming around as freely as possible. Pigs will make a mess of the turf where ever they go. This is why pigs are great for clearing woods; throw a few pigs into a wooded area and a couple of weeks later the ground will have been cleared, turned over and more fertile than ever.

The very next day after Alex had gone to school I went into town and went around all the pubs collecting their empty bottles. By lunchtime I had collected enough bottles, some peat, bags of cement and some sand. I was going to do six floors. By the end of that week I had built six pig houses by using corrugated sheets and wooden posts. After I had built the pig houses, I put the Victorian floors in. I was so impressed with myself; the pig houses looked great. Alex, Dan and Ken were all amazed at what I had done. "See, I'm not that useless after all," I said. Well it did not go all that well. I had a slight problem, while I was building the floor in one of the pens, I had somehow lost my mobile phone!

"Dan have you or Ken seen my mobile?"

"No," he said, "What, you haven't lost your phone in the cement," he said laughing.

"Yeah, funny, I am not that stupid."

Two hours later I still had not found it. "Dan, can you phone my mobile?" We all listened and we could hear it as we walked nearer to one of the pig houses.

Dan began to laugh, "Ken quick! Come here," he shouted, laughing. "Steve has only cemented his mobile into the floor."

"Oh! Knickers!" I said. Lucky I have a spare one as I was not going to dig the concrete floor up. Six months later all eighteen pens were finished and I had bought three British lop female pigs which were in pig and a massive boar called

Charlie. He was such a character. He was so strong you always had to keep an eye on him as he would want to play all the time and would come at you from nowhere and knock you flying. I never let Alex in with him or any of the boars as they could be a bit nasty. It was not worth the risk.

I had the two Mangalitzas from the pig course. I had another twenty Mangalitzas from another pig breeder. I had bought two large Blacks, two Berkshires and two Middle Whites. I had also rescued about sixteen pigs from a farm in Wales: a mixture of Tamworth crossed with another pig. Along with my other ten Saddleback pigs, I had within six months built up a large rare breed free-range pig farm operation.

During this period the three British lop female pigs gave birth which was an exciting time as I had never helped deliver piglets before. We had put the three female pigs in the pens nearest the house so we could keep an eye on them. We kept them separate from the other pigs so as not to disturb them. They were getting close to giving birth. Alex and I went out to see them all the time to see that they were all right. We sometimes just sat with the mums and rubbed their bellies which they seemed to like. They all seemed to be happy for us to be with them. I had been told that they can start to act odd just before they give birth.

Alex was outside and started to shout to me, "Dad! Come quickly." I ran outside and saw one of the females throwing plastic water butts about and smashing it against the pig ark. We watched for about an hour then she went into the pig ark and pushed the straw about and settled down. We both climbed into the pen and sat excitedly in the corner of the pig house. As we sat there, she started to breathe heavily. I watched as Alex moved forward and held her trotter stroking her side. "She seems to like that, Alex, keep doing it."

"Ok Dad!"

"Do you want a cup of tea?"

"Ooh yes please, Dad." I went into the house, and on coming back out I was amazed to see Alex picking up new born piglets and moving them round to the front of the pig so she could clean them. Alex looked at me with the biggest smile I had ever seen, she looked so happy. "Wow! Alex that's great, how many?"

"Two so far, Dad." I climbed into the pen and gave Alex her tea. We watched as one after the other the piglets were born. One of the piglets was born not breathing and I remembered what to do from the book. I picked the piglet up and stood up outside the pig house and started to swing the piglet between my legs and after a while it started to cough and then breathe.

"Wow! Dad, you saved it." Alex said.

About three hours later mother pig had finished. She had given birth to seventeen piglets, three had not survived but the others were all healthy and we were amazed to see that when they are born, their eyes are open and they can see and walk straight away. We put a pile of pig food just outside the pig house and left mummy pig suckling her piglets. We both walked into the house with big smiles hugging each other, we felt great.

We went through this two more times during that week and we had another twenty-seven piglets.

"Wow!" The place was awash with pigs. Word had got around we had piglets for sale but you are not allowed to take the piglets off the mum until they are eight weeks old and by then they were all sold. We had lost a few by the mums lying on them, which can happen. This can be prevented by sectioning off a corner of the pig house so mum cannot get in that corner but the piglets can. If you put a heat lamp over that area to keep it warm they can sleep, they then come out to feed off mum when hungry. As I had no electrics outside I did not have this option so just hoped we would not lose many. They all turned out to be pretty good mums and we did not lose anymore.

Things went well over the next few months, Alex was doing well in school and she was really enjoying her life on the farm. We had bought a large female Gloucester Old Spot which Alex had taken a strong liking to; we called her Rose. She had not been in pig for a couple of years, so was not able to be a mum. Rose became a mum and a good friend to Alex.

Then one day I was outside working and came to Rose's pig pen to find Alex inside the pig ark fast asleep with Rose. They were lying against each other. I left them there and went back an hour later and with a drink in hand I woke Alex up, she was so happy. I sat down next to her while we had our drinks and talked.

There was also another day when Alex had to have a day off school to help me. What happened was, Charlie the British Lop boar had decided to break out of his pen to go in search of the lush grass in the next field. Charlie was running all over the place and when you consider he was over twenty stone, then he was not easy to stop. Alex came out and spent the next four hours running all over the place. We could not help but laugh because whatever we did Charlie was not going to do what we wanted him to. We both sat eating a sandwich watching Charlie dig up our neighbour's field. Well we saw the funny side of it, but when our neighbour showed up he didn't, and had to spend a further hour trying to catch him.

Alex had an idea, "Dad?"

"Yes Alex?"

"Well, you know Charlie likes Rose and Rose will follow me anywhere. Why don't I take her for a walk to Charlie then see if he follows us back."

"Give it a go Alex," I said laughing not thinking it would work. My neighbour John and I sat there in amazement as Alex walked by with Rose and when Charlie saw Rose he came running over and followed Alex and Rose back to his pen. "Well done, Alex," we both shouted and clapped as she came by with a smile a mile wide. John helped me fix the pen and I helped him with his fence.

I was able to work from home most of the time and look after the farm when not doing my other job. I had also found a fruit and veg shop that threw out a couple of pallets of food a day. I had arranged to go on a Thursday and Saturday morning to collect this. The pigs loved the food. I gave them half of their normal pig food and made the rest up with fresh fruit and veg. They were just like kids leaving the greens until last and going after apples and grapes first. They loved the grapes and melons. This is how our days went on, Alex going to school then coming home riding her horse and helping me with the other animals.

My days were spent running the farm which was hard work but great fun looking after all the animals, letting the chickens out first thing in the morning. They had their own food. The llamas just wandered about the field feeding themselves, I just gave them some more hay and apples from time to time. The same went for the horses and the donkeys. The pigs went on as usual, feeding twice a day, giving them bedding, as the pigs were now on automatic water feeders, so there were no worries about them running out of water. Apart from the odd sick pig, which I dealt with as I had learnt how to inject them on the course and knew the signs when they were not well as the vet had showed me. The only other two problems I had was Charlie had decided to cut my leg with one of his sharp tusks, he cut through my leg like butter. I had gone into the pen to clean out his house. I always gave the males some food to keep them away from me while I'm cleaning it out. All was going well but as I brought back clean straw to put into his house and walked by him he just turned and nudged me with his tusk. It was my fault I got near to him while he was eating and he was just trying to shove me out of the way. I learnt from that mistake! I had to go to

Accident and Emergency as he had cut me down to the bone. I had to strap my leg up with masking tape as it was bleeding quite a lot. They stitched and glued my leg back together just in time for me to get Alex from school.

The other problem we had was one month we had a lot of rain and as we were on clay the ground did not drain very well, so the area got very boggy and the pigs were struggling to walk in it. Then one day when Alex and I were feeding the pigs, I was using a small dumper filled with straw, Alex was sitting in it. We were looking into one of the pens where we had seven young pigs. We were just about to start to give them some new bedding, when Alex said, "There are only six pigs." I looked and she was right but then we saw a large mound in the mud, we both jumped in and found that one of the pigs had died in the mud.

"Oh no, Dad," Alex started to cry as we pulled the pig out. I looked around the other pens and all the pigs were struggling. I made a phone call to a good friend called Andy and he came to the rescue. We both agreed they needed some sort of decking. I knew that down the road from me was a scaffolding company where they stored wooden planks. I phoned them and they said they would sell me some. I bought five hundred and with the help of Andy and another friend, within a week we had covered a good part of each pen with decking to keep the pigs out of the mud which they loved. I found out pigs like mud but they also like to get out of it too.

I asked Andy if he could put the drainage in for the road and the pens. He also constructed the automatic water system for each pen. Four weeks later all was complete and the pig area was a lot dryer. Andy helped a lot, also helping with the landscaping around the farm and other jobs; in all, he was there for six months. I thought he was moving in! We had a ginger pig on the farm that looked a lot like Andy as he was ginger too, and had the same looking face. Then one afternoon Andy was walking past Andy's pig pen and I shouted "Andy!" He looked 'round and Andy jumped onto the top of his fence to look over, they both looked down towards me side by side. I just turned away laughing my head off, as Andy walked away mumbling.

By the time Andy had finished all the work outside, the farm looked a lot different. I must say he did a damn good job and we all had a laugh or two while he worked. He also seemed sad to leave as I think he had grown attached to the pigs especially to Andy the ginger pig.

CHAPTER 6
WEST MID SHOW

Within six months I had become the largest rare breed, free range pig breeder in Shropshire. I had lots of other farms and smallholders contacting me to purchase piglets. One spring morning I was working on the farm when I had a phone call from the organizers of the West Mid show which was our county farm show. This was a large farming show where farmers and townies would go to see all types of farm animals on show. Along with loads of tractors, young farmer floats and loads of other entertainment and stallholders selling all types of products. This was held in Shrewsbury on the show ground.

They asked me if I would like to attend with a few pigs. There had been no pigs at the show for years and they wanted me to be the first to bring them back. They asked me to bring a large selection of pigs, eleven in all. They were even going to supply transport to get them there. Alex and I washed all the pigs that were due to go to the show. This was easier than we thought as the pigs seemed to like having a wash. We kept them in the barn overnight on fresh straw as it would make loading them a lot quicker.

Within three hours we had finished washing them and they were all bedded down for the night. We were not taking any boars as this could be dangerous to the public. One of every breed we had went to the show, along with Arthur and his mum. Arthur was a very young boar so did not pose a threat to anyone.

They arrived at 7am; it was going to take two trips to get them all to the show-ground and into the pens. We followed each load to the show-ground and helped off-load them on the bucket. You see, we moved all our pigs around the farm on the bucket. What I mean is we used pig food to get the pigs to do what we wanted. They would just follow us anywhere for food, this is how we had brought them up. By the time we had finished unloading them, a few other pig farmers had arrived with their pigs, but they used white pig boards to move their pigs around. The show organizers had decided to get a few other pig breeders to display their pigs at the show. They had also got a chap to do pig racing. "Can't wait to see that," I thought.

The show had opened and it seemed like everyone was making a bee-line for the pig displays as we were so busy. As Alex and I were sitting having a cup of tea, one of the organisers came over to us. "Steve, are you ready to display your pigs in the show ring later?"

"What?" I said.

"Yes, has no one told you, you have all your pigs entered into different pig show judging competitions during this afternoon?"

"Oh, my God!" I said.

"You have to move them into and around the ring using the pig boards."

"What?" said Alex, "we've never moved our pigs that way ever." After he left we both sat there just looking at each other not saying anything. Then after a few minutes silence Alex said, "What are we going to do, Dad?"

"Well let's just have a go," I said. "Will you help me, Alex?"

"Of course I will Dad, but we will need some boards and white coats."

"God, Alex you're right." We went over to the other pig

breeders at the show and asked if we could loan some coats and a couple of boards, which they were happy to help us with. We found that other pig breeders were very helpful and nice (some farmers can be right arsy).

Well, the time had come to take our first pigs into the ring. This is an area with a piece of rope 'round it where you take the pigs to and display them to the viewing public as you walk them around the ring. Alex had a white coat on which was an adult size, it went down to the floor and she had to roll her sleeves up. She looked at me and said, "What do I look like, Dad?"

"Great!" I said trying not to laugh. To be honest, her coat was too big and mine was too small. We looked like a right couple of wallies.

We opened the pen doors and started to move our first two pigs to the ring. As we made our way in, our two pigs caught a glimpse of the other pigs and took off towards them. No matter how much we used our boards they just ignored us and ran amok around the ring with me and Alex chasing after them shouting, "Here piggy piggy." The judges looked on with frowns as the people who were watching were doubled-up laughing.

The pigs were running around everywhere and running at

the other pigs, then the one I was trying to control made a bee line for the rope. It went straight under it and ran off towards the food tent. "Oh, my God!" I thought. "If she gets in there it will be a right mess." I ran faster and just as she entered the tent, I made a rugby tackle and brought her to the ground. With the help of two other people, we carried her back to her pen. Alex could be heard shouting, "Here, piggy piggy." But to no avail, she just kept doing her own thing around the ring. Twenty minutes later, both pigs were back in their pens. We sat down and looked at each other and burst out laughing. The judges agreed that the rest of our pigs could be judged from their pens. "I wonder why?"

The rest of the day went off without a hitch and we won a load of rosettes for our pigs and we even won some prize money. "Amazing," I thought. We ended the day watching the pig racing. "Wow!" I thought. "Pigs never seem to do what you want them to do." They were running everywhere except the direction they were supposed to go. At the end of the day we started loading with the help of some of the other farmers as they had got to know how useless I was at moving them. I was asked if I could reverse the trailer. "Yeah, I can do that," I thought. I jumped into the 4 x 4.

Alex said, "What are you doing, Dad?"

"I'm all right Alex, it will be fine," I said, as I started to reverse. Alex stood back as I went backwards. As I did, I could hear people shouting, "Stop!" I panicked and hit the accelerator going straight through the marquee and smashing down the pens holding our pigs. "Freedom!" they must have thought as they ran off across the show ground with everyone chasing after them. As I got out of the 4 x 4, I looked at Alex she just looked at me and walked away shaking her head and giggling to herself. By the time we had rounded all of the pigs up, loaded and transported them back to the farm which took two trips, it was 11 pm when we finally put the last pig to bed back on the farm. We waved good night to the driver and bunged him a tenner for all the help he had given us during the two days. "Night," we both shouted as he left.

I looked at Alex, "What a great day Alex, what did you think of it?" Alex looked at me and started to laugh, "It was so cool, Dad. Fancy a cuppa before bed?" Alex asked.

"I'd love one. I'll just put the chickens to bed." We sat down together in the lounge and talked about the day's events over our tea then hit the sack and slept soundly.

Our day to day routine went on as normal from then on, pigs being born left, right and centre. We also had a white Mangalitza piglet born. Being the only piglet in that litter, we called him Arthur. He was so cute and it seemed very easy to get him to do things, which was when I first realized how intelligent the breed was. Everything was normal, until the day Scarlett was born, and then everything changed.

CHAPTER 7
SCARLETT IS BORN

I was not looking forward to the day's events as today was when I had to take some pigs to slaughter. This is one part of running a farm I could never get used to. As we hand-rear every pig and get to know them all, we do get so attached to them. Alex and I made a point of not naming any of the pigs that were ear-marked for slaughter, so as to try and keep that closeness we had with them to a minimum.

The night before, I had marked the pigs that would be going to slaughter. The way this is done is by giving them a slap mark. I would feed them as usual and while they were eating I would slap them. By this, I don't mean I would go up to a pig and slap it across the face!

Each farm has a pig breeding number and when you take them to slaughter you have to mark them with that number.

You use a long handled bar which at one end has numbers that are made up of little metal spikes arranged to form your number which protrudes out of the bar. You dip the end of the bar into special animal ink marker and slap the pig on both shoulders. This does not hurt the pigs as their skin is very tough around this area. That is why I slap them while they are eating so they do not really notice. This has to be done so you know where the meat has come from.

Alex had been with me a few times and knew the whole process. I thought Alex should understand what happened and as Alex wanted to be a vet, I thought this was important. When I designed the pig run I had thought about how I would move the pigs from pen to pen and how I would load them into the trailer. When I was on my own this made loading them much easier.

On the day in question I had taken Alex to school and on arriving back at the farm, hitched the trailer up and drove over to the pig pens. I dropped the tail-gate and put some sheep gates around the back as the pigs would walk out of the pen and into the trailer. This system worked ninety per cent of the time and when it didn't, well put it this way, I would have to go and grab a cup of tea, relax and think of another way to load them which I always did, luckily this was not one of those days.

I had not fed them so as I opened the gate I shook the bucket and the pigs followed me up the ramp and I threw the food onto the floor. They all started to eat while I pushed the trailer door up quickly and secured it before they tried to get out. "Mmmm that was easy," I thought.

The biggest problem with pigs is they are very intelligent as they are the second most intelligent animal next to dolphins. The problem with this is that sometimes they seem to know what is going on. When I arrived at the abattoir I would be met by James, a really nice guy who took the welfare of the animals very seriously. The animals were all kept separately and would be led one by one to a room where they would be stunned out of sight of the other pigs and then killed while asleep. I always brought them here even though it was an hour's drive to Thomas's the slaughterhouse in Rhos near Wrexham. I knew if it had to be done, then this was the best place for that, all part of the process of being a farmer, but if there was any way I could make it easier for the pigs, I would.

As I arrived, I reversed to the door and dropped the gate and the pigs would just follow me to their pen. They were so trusting of me, that this got to me so much and James understood this and did his best to reassure me; he would make sure they felt nothing. I knew that if we did not eat these types of pig then we would lose all the rare breeds as no one would keep them as pets, well almost until I came along. I had taken five large white pigs (British lops) and it was sad to see them go. I got back into the car and broke down and just cried thinking, "I cannot keep doing this as it is so hard." James came out and sat with me and talked with me about why I was doing what I was doing. How without me breeding rare breed pigs they would just die out. I knew he was right, it was just so hard. I think he saw me as a bit of a soft sod, well to be honest he was right. I pulled myself together and headed back to the farm.

About an hour later, I was pulling back into the farm yard, unhitched the trailer after hosing it down and headed into the farm house. On the way, in I noticed the Mangalitza pig throwing her plastic tub around, "Mmmm, she is about to have her piglets," I thought. I went into the house, made myself a coffee and went outside. This was her first litter and I would stay on hand just in case she needed my help. Most pigs will have a litter of anything between twelve and seventeen piglets, Mangalitzas would only have six. They were born a lot bigger than the normal piglet so you did not tend to lose any as you would with the other breeds.

She lay down and started to get comfortable in the straw. I held her trotter and began to stroke her head. I had found that a pig likes you to hold her trotter, when giving birth, they love the company too. She started to moan and groan as she pushed the first piglet out. I moved it round to her head so she could lick it clean which she did instinctively. Piglets are born with their eyes open and can walk straight away, amazing to see and I never got bored watching and helping the pigs give birth. An hour and six piglets later she had finished. All six piglets had picked a teat and was drinking milk from their mother. Piglets will pick a teat and stick to it never moving to another one. The other fact I never knew is that they have two wombs either side of them. They would give birth two one side and then the placenta would come out and then the same with the other side. I did not have to get rid of this, as mummy pig would eat this. I gave her a load of pig feed and left her to it as she did look tired.

It was time to get Alex from school and as I drove to the school I thought about the day's events. How in the morning I had taken five pigs to the abattoir and in the afternoon six pigs had been born. Funny old life on the farm with the ending of one life and the start of a new one, just another normal day on the farm I thought. What I did not know, is that it would start to get weirder over the next few months.

As we were driving back to the farm I was telling Alex about the day's events. Last thing I told her was, "The

Mangalitza has had her piglets." I thought ending on a positive would be good.

"Wow!" Alex said, "can't wait to see them." We arrived home and Alex rushed upstairs to get changed out of her school uniform. We both went outside armed with a cup of tea. Alex was really excited as the only other Mangalitza that had been born on the farm was called Arthur. He was a white Mangalizta and his mum was called Marilyn. She was a very furry white pig, looking more like a sheep...that's why I called them shigs. We did not even know she was in pig (pregnant), but a couple of months after buying her she was 'round the back of her pig house and looked very unhappy. I remember it was a very wet and cold day and as I walked around the back of the pen I found a small piglet on the ground, muddy and wet. I picked him up and rushed into the house for Alex to look after while I carried on outside.

It was about two hours later when I finally got back into the house after feeding and bedding everyone down. As I went into the lounge, Alex was sitting on the sofa with the piglet in her arms fast asleep. Alex had cleaned him up. He had drank some milk out of a baby bottle and was very warm and contented now. I made the fire up and got one of the dog crates and filled it with straw. Sometimes you have to bring piglets up yourself for the first few weeks as the mother cannot cope with all of them. You feed them baby's milk as this is the closest you can get to pigs' milk. Arthur stayed in the house for the first two weeks and we took him out daily to spend some time with his mum to keep the bond between them. Alex did really well looking after him and when he finally went back to his mum it was like he had two mums from then on. Whenever Alex was around his pen he would come running up to her for a cuddle which is unusual for a pig as they do not like being picked up.

Now we had six more new Mangalitza piglets: three blondes, two swallow belly and one red. Over the next few weeks the weather was great. Alex would either be on the trampoline or in with the Mangalitza piglets. Every time we went into the pen, the red piglet would leave her mum to cuddle up and play with us. I started to notice the red piglet getting out of its pen and walking around. On the one afternoon I caught the red piglet watching Alex on her Trampoline. She sat there for about thirty minutes just watching her. This happened more and more until one day when she was about five weeks old.

It was early in November 2009, Alex and I had been outside feeding the pigs and were just going into the house for a drink. The weather was unusually warm for this time of year; there was not a cloud in the sky. We were in the kitchen drinking when we first heard the noise, it sounded like a little girl giggling. "Dad what is that?" Alex asked me.

"I'm not sure, Alex." We listened and waited to see if we heard it again and there it was. We got up and walked out of the door into the garden to be met with the weirdest thing we had ever seen.

There on the trampoline was the red Mangalitza pig. She was bouncing up and down clearing about four feet every time she bounced. "Wow!" I said.

"She must have got out of the pen and followed us back." said Alex trying not to laugh too much. Even after seeing us she did not stop, she just kept bouncing and giggling. The smile on her face was amazing to see. "She really does like it," said Alex.

We had been sitting there for about half an hour and she had not stopped bouncing. I looked at Alex and said, "Maybe she would like a go on the slide."

"What?" Alex said. "Dad, oh go on then, but how will she get up it?"

"Easy," I said, "we will use a plank of wood." Alex had a small child's slide and the plank fitted perfect up to it. I picked her up and walked towards the slide. I showed her the plank and helped her walk to the top. Even to this day I think she fell down it by accident letting out a squeal as she went. But on reaching the bottom she looked up with a big grin on her face, then ran around to the front of the plank, walked up it and went down the slide on her own, letting out another loud squeal. Alex was clapping and laughing so much; we both sat there for the next hour while she played on the slide and then onto the trampoline until she lay on top of it and fell asleep.

"Dad what are we going to do with her?" Alex asked.

"We will bring her into the house to live with us."

"What! You're joking," Alex said. As Alex said this she looked at me and walked off laughing shaking her head saying, "You're not are you?"

I picked her up carefully and lay her down on the settee. While this had all been going on the two dogs had looked on in disbelief. Now they were sitting in the front room with me, looking at this thing sleeping on the settee. Alex came downstairs and settled on the sofa with a drink. "So Dad what are you going to do with her?" she asked.

"I don't know Alex, what are we going to call her?" I said.

"I know! Scarlett, as she is red and that's her mum's name too."

"Scarlett…m'mmm…yes, that sounds good to me."

We had our tea, fed the dogs and Scarlett. They got on really well and the dogs seemed to accept her straight away. We let the dogs out to do their business and Scarlett followed. She watched them have a number one and two and she then copied them. From the very first day in the house she never made a mess on the floor. Scarlett even started to knock on the door with her nose to let me know when she wanted to go out. "I know Alex, I'm going to train her to do tricks and see if I can get her to go down a big slide."

"You are joking?" Alex said looking at me. "Oh my God, you're not, are you?"

"I'm also going to turn the downstairs' utility room into her bedroom, with a bed settee and TV for her."

"I'm off to bed Dad, you're mad."

"Night night, Alex."

That was it, the idea had been born and I was going to train Scarlett and make her one of the family. As we had been sitting there Scarlett had got onto the dogs' bed and curled up with the dogs. They didn't seem to mind at all, well, until she tried to suckle on their teats as they do have sharp teeth. The dogs made sure she did not do that again.

The next couple of weeks were pretty normal for me. My days were spent taking Alex to school, looking after all the animals and training Scarlett. Scarlett had now settled into her new room and in the evenings when she decided it was time for her bed she would get up and bang and her nose on the utility room door. I would open the door and she would go in, jump onto her bed and go to sleep. Sometimes I would curl up with her and we would fall asleep together watching TV as she had one in her room.

Scarlett was going on the trampoline and slide every day. We even had a small one in the house so she could play on in it the evenings. I had even trained her to open a door on command. Seemed like a good idea at the time until she went and opened the kitchen cupboards and ate a load of flour, pasta, cereal and whatever else she could lay her hands on. I could not tell her off as she sat there covered in white flour with a big grin on her face.

Scarlett was now going down a bigger slide and was used to walking on the lead. One very cold winter's morning, I decided to take Scarlett and the dogs for a walk across the fields. As we walked through the field we came across a large frozen layer of water. As we lived on clay the fields never drained that well when we had a lot of rain. Now in front of me was an area of about twenty square metres of frozen water but not too deep. As we walked around it, the dogs tippy toed onto the surface. Scarlett sat watching them for a while as they made their way slowly to the other side. All of a sudden, she stood up and tried to run across the surface. After a few feet, she fell and slid at great speed to the other side, again with a big smile on her face. She loved it. Then for the next hour I sat on the stump of a tree whilst watching Scarlett, Ruby and Cerys running across the ice and sliding on their bottoms. "I wish I had my camera," I thought. The dogs had watched Scarlett and had copied her. All three of them were enjoying it. When they started to look tired, I walked them back to the farm house. It was so cold so when we got back, I lit the log burner in the kitchen, made them all a cup of tea which they lapped up quickly, then they all settled down in front of the log burner for the afternoon. I had to go outside and feed the rest of the pigs; it had to be done.

Winter time on the farm was not much fun. Scarlett was not allowed contact with any other farm animals. She had been granted a free movement licence which meant she could go anywhere without restriction. She was the first pig ever to be granted this. When farming, all animals on the farm have to have a passport. You apply for this from a government organisation called Defra and you also have to contact your local authority. Once you have these numbers and letters, which show the area the animals live, whenever you move animals from place to place you have to fill in movement forms. Animals would have tags in their ears. Pigs would also have a tattoo on their shoulder. This is applied with a wooden paddle with small pins on it with your numbers and letters. You dipped the paddle in ink then slapped the pig on the shoulders. Pigs have very tough skin and I would slap them whilst they were eating so they hardly noticed. The rules are very stringent when it comes to moving animals that might enter the food chain. Defra has put in place the movement rules to prevent animals that may have a disease from contaminating other animals. It was agreed that Scarlett would never be eaten and was given a special licence which no other animal had been given, to go where ever she wanted. The one rule which could never be broken was that Scarlett could never mix with the other farm animals again.

I was now taking her to the park in Shrewsbury. I would drive over with Scarlett in her trailer to the park, unload her and walk around for about an hour with her on the lead at different times. As the weather got warmer there would be an ice-cream van there. We would go over and have a '99 Whippy'. Scarlett loved it. The people in the park would just stand with their mouths open pointing at me and Scarlett, stopping to stroke her. She loved the attention lapping up every minute of it. This was how life went on with Alex and me running the farm and Scarlett living in the house as one of the family.

News started to get around locally about Scarlett and me. We were being asked if we would go to schools and give talks about Scarlett and how she lived with us on the farm. The children and Scarlett loved it. I would take her into the room, and the children would all gather round stroking her and listening to me talk. Scarlett would just sit there loving every minute.

One Saturday I had a reporter from the local newspaper, around doing a write-up on the farm to do with the pig business I had set up. While I was talking to him about the farm, his gaze kept going towards the other side of the fence. Every now and again he could see this woolly pig appear above the fence line and then my daughter. You could hear what sounded like two children giggling. "What's that?" he cried.

"Oh that's my daughter playing with our house pig."

He laughed, "You have got to be kidding."

"No, I'm not," I said, and as I opened the gate, he walked into the back garden to be met with the sight of my daughter and a woolly pig playing on a trampoline. "That's nothing," I said, and at that, Alex got off the trampoline and Scarlett just carried on bouncing.

"No way," he said laughing. "I have to take a picture of this." He then got on the phone and started to tell someone over the phone what he was seeing. I could hear him saying, "Yes! Yes! …on a trampoline."

"She likes the slide too!" I said. At that I picked her up and put her by the slide. She ran up the plank to go down the slide, giving off a squeal.

"You will not believe what she is doing now," he said to the person on the phone. He hung up, took a few more pictures and shot off. He didn't mention anything about the article to do with the farm business.

The next morning, very early, we had a knock at the door. "Who could that be on a Sunday morning?" All I could think was that it may be Chris wanting a cup of tea. Chris was one of my neighbours who would come 'round for a natter after checking on his sheep. I came downstairs and opened the door to be met with about ten men with cameras. "We have come to see the pig," they said almost in unison.

"No way!" I said.

CHAPTER 8
THE PRESS ARRIVE

They introduced themselves. They were reporters from all the national newspapers. I was amazed how quick the news had travelled about Scarlett as it was only yesterday when the news broke about her. I invited them all into the house and made them a drink.

Alex came downstairs as she had heard all the noise. "Why are all these people here, Dad?" she asked.

"They have come to see Scarlett," I replied.

"Shall I get her?" she said.

"Yes, that's a good idea." At that, Alex went into the lounge.

One of the reporters said, "She's in the house?"

"Yes," I said. "Scarlett is in her bedroom at the moment."

"You're kidding!" he said.

"No! She lives in the house with us." Scarlett entered the room smiling and grunting.

"Wow! She's woolly," one of the reporters said.

"Scarlett will need a wee," I said opening the door and Scarlett went out for a pee and a poo. We all followed her outside.

After Scarlett had finished, they watched her in awe, as she walked towards the plank by the slide, walked up it and slid down the other side and she started to run 'round, doing it over and over again. None of them took out a camera. They all just stood there in disbelief.

"Do you want to see her on the trampoline?" I said. They all just stood there open-mouthed and nodded. I picked her up and walked towards the trampoline. As I got nearer to it, Scarlett wriggled free and landed on the trampoline with a large bounce. I stood back and watched as the press gathered around and took photos of her bouncing and giggling as she went higher and higher. They all just kept looking at each other in disbelief as they took loads and loads of pictures.

An hour later Scarlett was all worn out. I put her on the

floor; she had her breakfast and a drink then fell fast asleep in front of the log burner in the kitchen. The press asked me all about Scarlett and how this came about. They also wanted to know about Alex and me. Two hours later they were all gone.

Alex and I just sat at the breakfast table looking at each other. "Dad, did that just really happen?"

"Yes, I think it just did!"

"What a strange way to spend a Sunday morning," I said.

There was another knock at the door, "Oh, not another reporter," Alex said.

I went to the door and opened it. "Morning," came a voice. "Ha ha, morning, Chris," I said.

"What's so funny?" he said.

"Tell you later; come on in, the kettle is on." Chris came into the kitchen, settled down at the table and we told him all about the morning's events over tea and a bacon butty! Just kidding, we had toast.

Alex and I did not realise how weird our lives were going to get over the next few months, or how I would come up with ideas that always seem normal to me and still do, but for some reason, everyone else doesn't.

Two days later and Scarlett was on the front page of a lot

of the national newspapers and all over the internet. We carried on as normal; Alex went to school, I worked on the farm with all the animals and in my free time I trained Scarlett. By now, Scarlett could open doors on command and sit and lie down when told. She bounced on the trampoline which she loved, played on the slide and now could walk on the lead. I also had her in the garden and had trained her to go over jumps.

I wanted to find the biggest slide I could and get her to go down it. I found one that was about ten feet high. "Mmmm," I thought I would need to get a ramp built, so she could go up on it but that would have to wait for a bit.

One evening Alex had some music on the TV and Scarlett got up and started to bounce around the room. That's when we found out Scarlett liked music and could dance. She would go 'round and 'round in circles which Alex and her loved to do and it was great to watch.

It was now a couple of weeks since the press had been around and things had quietened down at long last, as the phone had been ringing non-stop, but then came 'the' phone call.

Early one evening we were all sitting in the lounge, dogs were curled up with Scarlett, Alex and I watching Harry

Potter on TV, when the phone rang. On answering it, I heard a voice say "Good evening, I work for Simon Cowell and we would like Scarlett to come onto our show, 'Britain's Got Talent'." I thought at first this was some sort of joke. We talked for about thirty minutes and it was agreed that Scarlett would be going to the NEC auditions in Birmingham. We decided instead of taking Scarlett we would video her and take that. They agreed that would do at this stage and if they liked what they saw, Scarlett would be going to the live event at Birmingham Hippodrome Theatre.

The NEC audition was only a month away and we had to make some sort of video. We decided to do a video of her life on the farm, living in the house with the dogs and us and of all the things she could do. We also made a video of me dancing in a Santa outfit with Arthur the white Mangalitz; don't ask why, it just seemed like a good idea at the time. Alex and one of her friends were in elf outfits. They had a dance routine and Arthur and I just seemed to wander round aimlessly in circles. When we watched the video back I could not believe what I was doing. I looked a right charley! "Oh well, in for a penny, in for a pound," I thought.

Four weeks later we went with the video to the NEC. Wow! It was so busy. There were all types of unusual looking people, from Leprechauns and someone who was sprayed gold to whole dancing troops. We both looked around to see if there were any other animals but we could not see any.

"I think we have to go over and register at that desk," Alex said.

"How do you know that?" I said.

She sighed, saying, "There is a big sign above the desk, saying 'Registration', Dad." She walked towards it muttering and shaking her head.

"What was that?" I said, with a smile on my face.

"Oh, nothing," she said giggling to herself. Alex was excited and we were meeting all sorts of different people. We queued to register and get our number. When we got to the desk we told them our names and said we were the Trampoline Pig Act. He looked at us with a smile of disbelief on his face. He leaned over to someone else and they said, "Oh yes, we are expecting you." They directed us to a large waiting lounge where other acts were waiting to audition. We did not have to wait too long before we went upstairs where we met a Producer of the show and they played the video.

They watched the video of me prancing around in a Santa outfit with a woolly pig running around me, while my daughter and her friend did a dance routine in front of me. Then it went to Scarlett in the house with the dogs and on a small trampoline. The producer stopped the video twice getting more people in to see it. They stood watching, laughing and some of them giving the occasional sideways look at me, probably thinking, what is this guy like? When the DVD had finished, they turned to us and said, "We would love to have her on the show. Do you know what Scarlett will be doing when you bring her?"

I did not know what to say. I tried to mutter something but all that came out was, "Uh?" from what they asked. Alex was starting to giggle and she nudged me in the ribs. "No! We had not thought of that," I said.

"Well, you had better go away and start getting something together as you will be there in a couple of months."

"Oh my God," I thought. "Ok!" We both said and left very excited. I looked at Alex, "Fancy going on the show with her?"

"You are joking!" she said.

"No! Let's think about what we could do." By the time we got home we had a very good idea of what we were going to do.

We had decided that Scarlett and I, along with Alex and a friend called Holly, would go on the show. We had come up with the idea that Alex and Holly would do a dance routine while Scarlett came on spinning with me dancing with her. Then while the girls carried on dancing, I would take Scarlett over about four to five jumps up a plank to the top of the slide and then she would slide down onto a trampoline and bounce on it, ending up with her jumping off, running forward with me to end up between the two girls with Scarlett jumping into my lap on cue as they stopped dancing.

Alex phoned her friend Holly to ask her if she would be interested in going on the show. "Really," she said not believing what Alex had just told her. I had to go on the phone and talk to her mother so they would believe us.

"Wow! That will be great fun," Holly's mother said. I explained about what we would be doing and all the rehearsals we would need to do. She said that would be fine. The next day we picked Holly up and brought her over to the farm to show her what we were going to do. Alex went upstairs with her to discuss and practice some dancing while I went outside to train Scarlett over jumps.

A few days later I was sitting in the kitchen with Alex. "We need help doing this, Dad," Alex said. I hated to admit it but she was right. The training was coming along, but how we were going to set out the whole routine was the problem. Alex came up with the idea of getting the help of a dancing teacher.

So, a week later we had the help of a dancing teacher from Adcote School and we were allowed to use one of the halls to practice in. I had also asked the Rowton Castle Country Club where Alex and I were both members. This is where we would go to swim and they had a great dance studio. They had agreed to let us take Scarlett there and use the room free of charge to practice the routine. Every time we were in the dance studio practicing, members of the club would just stand there in disbelief. After we had finished rehearsals we would always pop into the main bar area for everyone to meet Scarlett. Scarlett loved the attention and always took everything in her stride. Darrel, the club manager was great with us.

I had known Darrel for twenty years and he had been at the club all that time and nothing was ever too much for him, but I do think I pushed him to the limits with Scarlett. I did think of asking Darrel if I could get Scarlett to swim in the pool and we could video her as I had remembered that in China they run a thing called the Pig Olympics where they held swimming races. So I thought of asking him if we could get her in the pool and have her jumping in, off a diving board.

"Mmmm," I thought. "How was I going to get her to do this and what would Darrel say?" I decided not to ask him as

I thought I would be pushing it and he had done enough already. I also thought he would think I was nuts.

The week went by rapidly; the girls had learnt the dance routine and Scarlett had learnt to dance, go over the jumps, run up the ramp down the slide and jump on the trampoline. She was very good. She only needed to poo and wee a few times in the dance studio, but I kept that from the owners of Rowton and Darrel. We had to string the whole thing together now.

It was one Sunday afternoon when we all arrived at Rowton Castle with Scarlett. All of the jumps, slide, trampoline and other equipment were all set up ready. The music we had all rehearsed to was ready. We started to go through the routine, slowly at first and a bit disjointed but things started to come into place. The manager, staff and club members had gathered to watch and would just stand there with mouths open wide in disbelief watching, not knowing what to think or say. I think they thought I was a bit 'out there'.

I have always thought myself to be fairly normal, though. When I was 18 years old I went to the USA for a three week holiday and stayed with my mother's friends. They had a son the same age as me and we had a great time. While I was there I went to a large shopping mall with Glen. On arriving we went straight into this shop where you could buy rockets, explosives, yes, dynamite off the shelf along with detonators. "Wow!" I thought. "Let's buy some and blow something up."

Glen looked at me saying, "No, let's buy a rocket and launch it!"

I sighed, "Oh! Ok then," I said. We bought a rocket launching pad, explosives and detonators. We went back to his place and built the rocket and launched it a fair few times as it had a parachute that exploded out at about 1000 feet.

"This is great!" I said to Glen. While he carried on building the next rocket to launch, an idea came into my head, but I kept it to myself.

Three weeks had gone past and I had seen a lot of California which is where they lived. It was the day before I was due to fly home and I said I wanted to pop back to the mall and do some shopping. They dropped me off and said they would come back in a few hours to get me. "Fine," I said as I would not need more than two to three hours. As they left, I shot off to buy a large suitcase. After buying this, I went to buy a few sweaters and jeans, just enough to cover them. I then headed to the store that sold the dynamite. I filled the case with dynamite, detonators and a rocket with launcher, I did not really need it though. I must have had about 200 sticks of dynamite, which I carefully packed into the suitcase.

When they collected me from the mall they said, "Wow! You have bought a lot of clothes."

"Yes I have, but I'm not going to open the case and show you, as it's all tightly packed."

"No worries," they said laughing.

I said goodbye the next day and pulled my two suitcases to the departure gate. I boarded the plane and arrived back in the UK after an eleven hour flight. My father was meeting me from the plane. As I walked towards him, he looked at me with my two cases and laughed, "My God, son you have bought a lot of clothes."

"No Dad, it's not clothes, it's dynamite," I said with a smile on my face.

"What?" he said.

"Yes, I've bought a case full of dynamite back with detonators."

"What? You are joking!" he said with a frown on his face.

"No really," I said.

"You could have brought the plane down with them!"

"Oh!" I said, the realisation of what I had done had just struck home with me. "God, Dad I did not think of that.

"Let's get you out of the airport before someone asks to see inside your case." We walked to the car with my dad pulling the case of dynamite shaking his head and chuckling and talking under his breath.

"Dad, be careful you're pulling the one full of explosives," I said trying not to laugh.

"Sod off," he said. We got in the car and started to drive back to my father's house. He looked at me, "Whatever made you think of bringing dynamite back with you?"

"Well, it seemed like a good idea at the time and you can buy anything out there." We spent the rest of the journey home talking about my holiday and I was making sure I did not bring the subject of rockets and explosives up again. We arrived at my father's house and walked into the lounge.

"Go on then, open it," he said. I unlocked the suitcase, and as I pulled the case open my dad's jaw just dropped. "Oh my God, how much is in there?" he said.

"Not that much," I said. He walked off into the kitchen and poured himself a glass of whisky. "Mmmm," I thought, never having seen my father drink before. "Not having tea?" I said, which was his favourite drink.

He just looked at me and said, "Stupid boy."

A few years later I put that dynamite to some good use! Well, I thought so. I was living in Machynlleth at the time and just as you went in on the left, was a small quarry. Well, one sunny afternoon for some reason the dynamite popped into my head. "I know! Why don't I see how big an explosion I can make?" I got together quite a lot of dynamite and a few detonators and walked to the old quarry. On arrival I spied a gigantic boulder in the side of the cliff that seemed to have a small gap behind it. I proceeded to push the dynamite firmly into the gap with anything else I could find and pushed the detonators into the dynamite. I connected a long piece of detonator wire which was about 4 metres long, which I thought was long enough. I took cover and connected the wire to the detonator switch. It was now early evening about 7pm. When I tripped the switch, nothing happened. I stood up, walked a bit nearer to have a look, I bent down and wiggled the wire. At that, there was an almighty explosion which blew me off my feet. I looked up to see a large boulder flying through the air. "Wow!" I thought, as it landed a few hundred feet away, crashing through someone's garage roof. Oh my God, I just sat there thinking what I should do. At that, I could hear sirens and could see a fire engine and a police car coming up the road. I quickly gathered the rest of my stuff, rammed it into my ruck sack and took off across the fields. I ran the long way home diverting by a few miles, until I reached the safety of our house and stayed in the rest of the evening. I wish I had kept some, as I could have used it on those two trees at the farm house, then they would have come down.

Well, getting back to the training and Scarlett. Now, where was I, oh yes, two hours later and we had cracked it, every time we went through the routine it was near enough perfect and everyone, even Scarlett, was enjoying themselves. The last time we did it, we got a loud applause from everyone watching. The noise did not seem to bother Scarlett at all. Everything was set. We were ready for the big day.

CHAPTER 9
BGT

The day had come. We were all up early as we had to be at the theatre in Birmingham by 10 am. I had hired a transit van which was loaded with all the equipment and a very large dog cage for Scarlett to travel in. We had breakfast and set off. Scarlett was used to travelling in her pig trailer and being in the back of the van made her travel sick. By the time we had got to Birmingham, Scarlett was a right mess. They had a special ramp at the back of the Hippodrome Theatre which we drove onto. We were lowered onto the back of the stage. I had always wondered how they got all the props back stage. We were going to meet Alex's friend Holly there with her mum.

I was at the back with Alex cleaning Scarlett up, when I

heard the voices of two men that I recognised, coming towards us. I heard Alex say, "Oh, my God, it's Ant and Dec." I turned 'round to be met by them both. "Hi there, Ant and Dec, this is Alex and I am Steve." "How are you both?"

"We are great, thanks," they replied. "How was your journey?"

"Yeah, ok, Scarlett had travel sickness but apart from that she is fine." They walked up to take a closer look at Scarlett.

"Wow! That's a funny looking pig," Ant said. Well I think it was Ant, I always get them mixed up. "Would you like to take a look at the stage and see the area you have to work on?"

"Yes," I said. "That would be great, Dec." Or was it Ant? I was thinking to myself.

Alex came with me and we walked onto the stage. "Wow! It is big," said Alex.

"Don't worry about it Alex, just think that we are back at Rowton Castle." But even as I was saying that to her, I had a hard job to believe it myself; to be honest I was bricking it. We started to talk to the back-stage crew and they helped us set up the jumps, slide and small trampoline. We had not been able to bring the one from the garden Scarlett normally used, as it was too big.

I went to get Scarlett. She was still looking a bit sick as we went onto the stage. She was slipping all over the place, the surface was too slippery for her. "Oh, hell, what can we do about the floor?" I said.

The crew moved all the jumps and other stuff from the stage and put a rubbery surface down. "Ok, let's set everything back up again." The new rubber flooring was better but she was not happy with the smell and feel of the rubbery surface. That's the only problem with animals like pigs, as they will do things when they want to, if they don't, then they won't and any little thing can upset them.

Alex and I went through the routine, trying to get Scarlett to go over the jumps and down the slide, but she was not having any of it. I was starting to get worried, as I did not want to go on stage and look a right wally.

It was getting close to the opening of the show. Outside was a long queue and the producers asked us if we could take the pig for a walk, so they could film her. They wanted Scarlett and me, to walk up and down the queue of the waiting public. Scarlett just seemed to take it in her stride as everyone crowded round her, wanting to stroke her. Then we went back inside, I settled Scarlett down and she fell fast asleep.

The show started. We had been there for about seven hours now and Scarlett was pretty fed up. I was back stage watching the different acts going on; there were a few funny sights to be seen. The one thing that I do remember was seeing an old man dressed as a Leprechaun, he went on, did a funny dance and got three yes's. I know I like green but he took it to a whole new level. Ant and Dec were by the side stage talking to each act before they went on. We were two acts away from going on. Alex and Holly were talking with Ant and Dec, they were all sitting on the floor together talking like mates, and they really put the girls at ease.

The Judges that evening were Amanda Holden, Piers Morgan and Louie Walsh. It was the night when Simon Cowell was ill, which was a shame as we knew he loved animal acts, so we would have been sure of a yes from him.

It was our time to go on. What we wanted to do was just have Alex and Holly go on, talk to the judges and then get ready to start the routine. I would come on with Scarlett as a surprise in the routine. We were talked out of this as they said the girls might be buzzed before I went on with Scarlett. We should have stuck to our original plan as it would have been better. We were told we only had a minute and a half but in fact we could have had three minutes, had we known this, we could have put together a longer routine.

We all went on together to talk with the judges, then we got ready to start. I went back to the side where Ant and Dec were. The music started and we were off. Scarlett started spinning and came to the front of the stage, then we went off to the jumps, she jumped three but knocked over the others, she went up the ramp and down the slide, onto the trampoline where she tried to jump, but it was a lot firmer than the one she had at home. Scarlett jumped off, I tried her over the jumps again, she jumped a couple and then went to the front to finish, with Alex and Holly side by side. Things did not go too well, it could have been a lot better. Alex and Holly were perfect, but oh well, we had to laugh.

The judges started to talk. Amanda Holden did not seem impressed, she said "I would go up a slide for a chocolate," this was how I got Scarlett to do her tricks, by giving her treats. I thought "Mmm…how many pigs have you ever seen doing that?"

Piers loved it and had nothing but admiration for us and he was amazed at what Scarlett could do, so he gave us a yes and Louie said, "Mmm... no, maybe next time, she needs to practice more." This would be hard as Scarlett would be a lot bigger, about five times bigger. I tried to get Louie to change his mind but he was not having any of it.

We left the stage and the girls burst into tears running to the back of the stage. They sobbed their hearts out. Scarlett and I walked to the back and she was wondering what all the fuss was about. The guy that does the 'after show' had come to interview us, but to be honest I was more interested in helping make the girls feel better, which I did not think went down too well with the chap, even his jokes fell on deaf ears.

An hour later they were okay and we were all packed up to go. Holly's mum had been backstage to collect her so it was just the three of us now. I looked at Alex and we both laughed and hugged each other. "Fancy a 'Mackie D's' on the way home?"

"Oh yes please," Alex said.

Scarlett was fast asleep in the back of the van, as before she was just wondering what all the fuss was about. Before we got in the van, Alex ran over to Ant and Dec and gave them a cuddle. They smiled and hugged her back. I shook their hands and thanked them for all their help. I turned to Alex and said, "They are really nice." We hugged each other and got into the van, we waved goodbye as our lift took us up to the outside. On the way home we talked about the day's events and carried on while we were eating our Big Mac, not really believing what had happened that day, not knowing things were going to get even crazier.

We arrived home quite late and unloaded Scarlett. She was so happy to be home running flat out around the garden. I opened the door to let the dogs out and they joined in. Now all three were running around and playing in the moonlight. Alex and I went into the house to make a cup of tea, ten minutes later we went outside with our drinks and they were all still running around and churning up the grass. Finally they came into the house and settled down together on Scarlett's bed. We also settled down and fell into a deep sleep.

CHAPTER 10
PET NATION FILMING

It was a couple of days later when we got the call from Sky One's Pet Nation. They wanted to come and film Scarlett, not doing her normal stuff, but dancing. "Ok!" I said, without thinking what I was agreeing to. I agreed they could come and film a week later. After putting the phone down, it suddenly hit me Scarlett could not dance.

Later that day I went to get Alex from school. "Hi Alex, Sky One's, Pet Nation are coming to film Scarlett dance next week," I said.

"What? Dad, she can't dance!"

"Yeah, I know that's the problem."

Alex sat there laughing and shaking her head and said, "Only you could agree to that, what are you going to do?"

"Well I am going to have to teach her to dance!"

We arrived home. I started cooking tea, whilst thinking how I was going to do it. After tea I went on the internet and found a guy in America who trained animals; he used a stick as a pointer. I watched for about an hour and thought, "Yes that's the way I will teach her to dance."

I went down to the cellar and found a long black metal stick, not sure what it was for but thought, this would do as a pointer. I went to the kitchen and got the grapes as this was Scarlett's favourite treat. I started by pointing at the end of the stick and when she put her nose on it I gave her a grape. I did this over and over, then I started to point at items like the table and door, when she touched her nose on it I gave her a grape. She began following the end after a couple of hours. I now started to move the pointer around in a circle and she would turn with it and then around me and she followed. All was going amazingly well. A few hours later I stopped using the pointer and just held a few grapes in my hand and she followed my hand.

Two days later I had Alex sitting in the front room with me waiting to see what I had taught Scarlett. I turned the music on, and off we went. I had Scarlett spinning around in circles and around me. I had her jumping up and sitting on her back. Alex just sat there with her mouth wide open and laughing. "Wow! Dad this looks so cool." Scarlett really seemed to like what she was doing, even when I had stopped moving my hand she carried on dancing to the music. The two dogs just sat there watching Scarlett dance. I looked at them and said, "I couldn't get you two to do that, you lazy pair." All I got back was a cheeky grin and "Woof, woof, woof." Ruby and Cerys just raised their heads, then lay back down.

It was a few days later when the TV crew and presenter of the show arrived for the filming. They took an hour to set everything up, the lighting had to be just right, they moved it so many times and I could not see any difference to when they first set it up an hour earlier. Oh well, we were ready at last.

The presenter wanted to know where Scarlett was. I told him, "She is outside playing." He looked at me with a funny look. At that I took him outside to find her playing on her slide, we stood there and watched her running up the ramp, down the slide with a small squeal coming from her. She was playing this game over and over again. "She loves her slide!" I said to the presenter, who was just watching with his mouth open. "What's wrong?" I said, "Haven't you seen a pig playing on a slide before?" I walked back to the house with a slight chuckle. "Scarlett," I called and she came running up into the house. The presenter had not said a word, then began laughing.

"I have never seen anything like that, where has she gone?" he said.

"Probably, to her bedroom, to watch TV."

"What?" he said.

"Follow me." We walked into her bedroom and there she was watching TV. "How did she turn it on?" he asked.

"Turn it off," I said, and as he did, Scarlett jumped off her bed went to the TV and pushed the button with her nose to turn it back on. I had taught her how to do this with the pointer stick.

We were now ready to film Scarlett dancing. The camera was ready and I turned the music on. Off she went jumping from the bed as she heard the music. Scarlett was great, she performed for the camera, spinning and dancing this way and that. All the way through the filming she was jumping and would spin to the left and then to the right while the music was going. Scarlett was not going to stop. We were at long last finished; we had been at it for about two hours and had so many takes, I cannot remember. We sat there talking afterwards and they were in a bit of disbelief with what they had actually captured on film.

"Thank you for everything," they said as they packed up to go with a bacon sandwich in hand. Scarlett just crashed out on her bed and fell fast asleep.

It was time for me to get Alex from school, so I actually left the same time as the film crew, whilst I left Scarlett sleeping in her bedroom. "How did it go?" Alex asked as she got into the car.

"Really well. Scarlett loved every minute of it. They said it should go out on Sky One in about a month." When we arrived home Alex went into Scarlett's bedroom and settled down with her to watch TV. When I looked in, Alex was trying to do her homework, while Scarlett was pulling everything out of her bag. It was so funny watching Alex, as fast as she was putting things back in, Scarlett was pulling them out.

"I think you should come into the kitchen to do your homework." I said laughing.

"Yes, I think you are you right, Dad."

While Alex was doing her homework, the phone rang. On answering, I heard, "Is that Mr Howell, the owner of Scarlett?"

"Yes" I said.

"Hi, we would like you to bring Scarlett to appear on The

Alan Titchmarsh Show in two weeks' time.

"Really?" I said, asking, "can I bring my daughter with me too?"

"Yes, no problem."

"Ok, what do we need to do?"

"We will send you all the details in the post today, but here are my contact numbers."

I came off the phone. "Alex?"

"Yes, Dad?"

"You will need a day off school as we are going to take Scarlett onto The Alan Titchmarsh Show in London.

"What is she going to be doing, Dad?"

"Oh, I don't know, Alex, I forgot to ask them that."

"Ha ha, what are you like, Dad?" Alex said.

CHAPTER 11
THE ALAN TITCHMARSH SHOW

Two weeks later, Alex and I were sitting at home waiting to see Pet Nation on Sky One, as Scarlett was going to be on that evening. As the show started, we settled down with our cups of hot chocolate in hand. Scarlett and the two dogs were curled up together in front of the log burner and one of our farm cats was curled up on the window sill.

The show started and fifteen minutes in, we were on; we both sat there laughing at how they had put the item together. Scarlett just lifted her head to look when she heard the music then lay back down. "That's what she thought of it, Dad," Alex said giggling.

When it had finished we looked at each other. "Well that was fun to watch." I said. "Now we have got to go and do it all again on The Alan Titchmarsh Show."

They had sent us all the details about what time they wanted us there, where to go, which was the main BBC building in London, what to wear, a pass to get through the main gate and details of what they wanted Scarlett to do. They were doing an animal section which was to show how talented animals can be. We had to get there for about 10 am, which meant we had to leave very early at about 4.30 am. We were going down on Monday morning which was just four days away.

Over the next couple of days we had so many phone calls. We had a phone call from a show in Korea, they wanted to come and film Scarlett at home. We had a call from a BBC show that wanted to spend the week with us filming which I was not totally sure what it was about but the show was going to be called 'Be My Guest'. I had said yes to all of them not knowing really what I was agreeing to. We had also more press arriving at the house over the next few days to take more photos, even Hello Magazine wanted to come and take photos. It was starting to get a bit crazy, I thought.

It was now Sunday evening and Alex was going to bed early. The pig trailer had been cleaned and filled with fresh straw for Scarlett's journey. I had filled four, one litre bottles with water for Scarlett. We had food for Scarlett and a couple of dog bowls for her to use. Alex and I had got plenty of snacks and drinks for the trip, so all was well. I had even thought of putting the DVD player in and a load of films to stop Alex getting bored on the way down.

I had programmed the Satellite Navigation so we would be able to find the BBC Television Centre. It was on the far side of London. I was going to wake Alex up when I had loaded Scarlett and all the items we needed for the trip.

The alarm went off at 3.30 am. I jumped out of bed and headed for the shower, I had always been good at getting up. After showering and getting dressed, I threw a couple of cups of coffee down me and a piece of toast. I woke Scarlett, which she was not too happy about, as it was way too early for her. I opened the back door and she reluctantly went outside. Scarlett was not outside long, as it was a chilly morning. I put her harness on which always excited her, as she knew that something interesting was going to happen. Once the harness was on, Scarlett ran excitedly around the kitchen table making a barking noise; the dogs were also getting excited. By now there was such a noise emitting from the kitchen. Surely that has woken Alex, I thought. I went upstairs with a cup of tea and toast in hand for Alex, not noticing Scarlett and the dogs following me up the stairs. Alex was still fast asleep, "Alex, time to get up," I said. She slowly started to stir. Alex had never been that good in the morning. "Come on Alex, you must get up, we have to get going, I have some tea and toast for you."

I was thinking, "I am never going to get her out of bed." Before that thought had even left my head, Scarlett and the two dogs barged past me and jumped onto Alex's bed pushing her off the other side onto the floor. I left her there screaming "Dad! Dad! Get them off me," I walked back downstairs, while they licked her to death, chuckling to myself and shouted back to her, "Bet you will get up now."

"Oh Dad, I hate you." I heard her shouting at me, then I listened standing halfway down the stairs and she soon started to laugh and talk to them all. I heard Alex saying to them, "Well at least I do not need a wash now."

A few minutes later I heard the dogs and Scarlett bombing down the stairs followed by a disgruntled daughter. "Morning Alex," I said laughing. "How are you?"

"Knickers!" she replied, which made me laugh even more. After a couple of minutes Alex started to laugh too. "We really need to get going, I will load Scarlett, while you get ready, there's some toast for you, now hurry up, oh, you have already had some, no worries, I will give it to Scarlett and the dogs." They ate it in seconds of seeing it. I put the dogs in the back garden, as I did not want them to see me get a lead, as they would have wanted a walk. We had a friend coming over for the day to look after the dogs and the rest of the animals. While they were out the back, I put Scarlett's lead on and led her to the trailer. The pig trailer we used was great, not too big, ideal for driving through London and perfect for Scarlett as she had plenty of room in it for her to spread out. Scarlett walked on eagerly anticipating the day's events. I closed the back of the trailer and went back inside to get Alex. "Are you ready?" I shouted.

"Yes, nearly," came the reply. I gave the dogs a treat, made sure they had water and settled them down. Our friend would be over soon, so I knew all the chickens would be let out and the dogs would be well looked after. I had made a list of what feed the animals all needed and the quantity, so I knew all would be well while we were away for the day. "Off we go," I said to Alex as we closed the front door. Alex settled herself down in the back of the car. She had the DVD player on already and was just picking a film. "What are you going to watch?" I said.

"Babe!" she replied.

We pulled out of the farm and headed for the M54, then the route we were going to take was M6, M5, and then M40 into London. Then around on the M25 with all being well, we would not get too much traffic. Even the M25 was flowing well with not too many hold ups, but then we hit the road off the M25 into London and we crawled all the way in. It took us a further hour and a half to get to the Television Centre. We arrived at 11 am, an hour late. "Late as always Dad," Alex said.

"Oh, fiddle-sticks," I said.

As we pulled up at the gate, I showed the Guard our pass, "Oh you're the guy with the pig. They told me about you," he said.

"All good, I hope," I said, laughing. He just looked at me and directed us around to the back. We parked up and walked through a door saying 'stage door', and we were greeted by a floor runner... I think that is what you call them. I told him who we were.

"Oh, great," he said, "We have been waiting for you, we were getting worried."

"The last stretch into London took us ages."

"We have Katherine Jenkins and John Barrowman here today," he said.

"Wow! John Barrowman out of Torchwood, he's great," Alex said.

"Who's he?" I said.

"Oh, Dad you don't know him?" We were walking along the side of the stage, behind the curtains and we could hear someone singing. As we turned the corner we saw a man singing. "That's John Barrowman." Alex said.

We stood listening to him rehearsing, and after a while I asked, "Can I leave Alex with you, while I check on Scarlett?"

"Yes sure, she will be fine with us." I went back outside to the trailer.

I had to wake Scarlett as she was fast asleep. "Scarlett!" I called. She started to stir and when she saw her lead, she got excited. I grabbed a few doggy poo bags and took Scarlett for a walk around the back of the studio. Scarlett had a good sniff around, did her business quite a few times so the poo bags were very full by the time we headed back to the trailer. Luckily there was a bin where I could deposit the bags. I gave Scarlett some water and food which she enjoyed. There was an area at the back of the studio where we could practice. Scarlett was great, dancing and spinning, doing everything I asked of her; this was going to go well, or so I thought.

We had been practising for about half an hour, so I decided to give Scarlett a rest. We walked to the back of the trailer and she walked in and settled down for a rest. I closed the back up and headed back inside to see what was going on.

When I arrived back inside the studio, they were filming Katherine Jenkins. As they did two shows a day, one was recorded before a live audience and one was completely live. I looked for Alex, she was nowhere to be seen. I looked at the floor manager and was about to ask where Alex was, "Don't you worry," he said. "She is fine. Alex is back stage having tea with John Barrowman." A few minutes later Alex appeared with a big grin on her face and a CD in her hand.

"Having fun?" I asked.

"Yeah, great Dad, he was so nice we sat and talked and he gave me a signed CD. What a great guy; thanks for bringing me, Dad."

"How's Scarlett?"

"She is surprisingly well, and doing everything I asked of her."

"Great, should go well then," Alex said.

"Famous last words," I thought.

We sat and watched the recording of the next day's show. After lunch we were going to be called. I was starting to get very nervous and could not eat anything. "Dad," Alex said. "Look over there, they are scattering something on the stage." We looked in disbelief as they scattered nuts.

"No, it's corn," I said to Alex.

"Oh, great," Alex said. "I bet Scarlett will love them."

"Oh, knickers, you're right she will want to eat them." Not long after, I was asked to get Scarlett and as we approached the stage I could see Scarlett start to sniff the air. "Oh, heck!" I thought. Alan Titchmarsh started the show by walking on with Scarlett on the lead which went well, she did as she was told, but I saw that she had clocked the corn. Later on in the show we were asked on and Scarlett was supposed to dance. As the music started I took her off the lead and she went straight for the corn instead of dancing, taking no notice of me or the music, Scarlett just wanted to fill her face. It got a good laugh from Alan and the audience. We left the stage and I took Scarlett back to her trailer, I settled her down with some water, but did not feed her as she had eaten so much corn.

I went back in to find Alex and as I approached her she was shaking her head, laughing. "Well that went well," she said, grinning from ear to ear.

"Oh shut up," I said, laughing. "Let's watch the rest of the show." After it had finished we were asked if we would like to go into the green room for some refreshments.

"Oh, what is that?" I asked.

"It is where all the guests and the stage crew go when the show has finished, for food and drinks and just a general natter," they told me.

"Yes, that would be great," Alex said, before I could reply. We went in and got some food and something to drink. They had everything...all types of drinks and Champers to boot.

"Oh, I wish I wasn't driving," I thought. Alan Titchmarsh entered the room and some of the other guests and Alex and I, had a good chat with him, then he sat talking with Alex, as I talked with the floor producer about the making of the show. About two hours later we were on our way out of the television studio. As we went through the gates, I looked at Alex and we both burst out laughing. "Well that went well," I said giggling.

"Yeah, right!" Alex said. Ten minutes later Alex was fast asleep. It took us about five hours to get home and she slept the whole of the journey. When we arrived home I unloaded Scarlett. "Leave everything else," I said to Alex. "Let's just get into the house and get to bed." Alex went straight upstairs. "Night, Dad," she said.

"Night, Alex." I went into the lounge with Scarlett, sat on the settee where she joined me. I fell fast asleep with Scarlett curled up next to me.

CHAPTER 12
A FRIEND LIKE ME

It was a morning like any other; all the pigs were up and about eating the food I had put out. Fruit, veg and sugar beet was the order of the day for them. The horses, donkey and miniature pony had their hay and carrots. The llamas were chomping away on a couple of buckets filled with apples along with the odd piglet that had got out of their pens, which was the norm. The chickens were tucking into corn that I had strewn all around the pen. I wanted them to peck away at the ground which was good for them for the nutrients. I had collected all the eggs: 14 eggs from 12 hens was amazing. I had been over to the sheep pulling open a bale of hay for them, making sure all the water butts were filled.

It was now just after 9 am and all the morning's work had been done. I sat down on the front patio with a cup of tea in hand. I heard a noise in the garden, it was a small barking noise which was getting louder.

"Oh, you're up, are you?" I shouted. I walked to the back garden gate, opened it and there was Scarlett walking around the garden. She had sleep in her eyes, her nose deep into the ground digging at the grass. Scarlett saw me come through the gate, ran over to me jumping up.

"Ok, you can go on it." I picked Scarlett up and put her on the trampoline and left her bouncing whilst I got her breakfast ready. The two dogs came out of the kitchen, sat down as they did, watching Scarlett bounce. I thought I could see the one dog's jaw dropping whilst she shook her head.

I went into the kitchen chuckling to myself. As I made them all breakfast I could hear even more noise. As I went into the garden, they were all on it jumping around like three children. I laid the food down by the trampoline, but not one of them came off to eat it. "What are you all like?" I said, giving them all a cuddle. "I'm off to get a fresh cuppa, see you later." I called, as if they knew what I was saying.

With tea in hand I settled back down onto the bench at the front of the house. Looking up the field, I spied a large tree. This tree was starting to wind me up, the branches were hanging down over one of the gates I used to move the pigs through. It was making it virtually impossible to use this gate.

I don't know if I have told you already? But years ago, my first job at the age of 16 was to work for some forestry guys. I had to get up at 4 am, meet them at the end of a road…a mile's walk. They picked me up at 5.30 am and brought me home at 6 pm. It was such a long hard day! My day was spent using a small chainsaw to take the branches off the trees that the guys had taken down. I remember the one day they told me if I climbed a tree to the top, I would have a great view across the valley. Yep, I climbed the tree and you guessed it, they started up their chainsaws, cutting it down while I was up it. I started to scream but instead of the tree coming down swiftly, the tree came down like a feather. The trees in the forest were tightly packed, which did the trick in slowing the fall. It was probably the hardest job I have ever had. After two weeks, I had to pack it in.

Getting back to my problem on the farm…this damn tree, I thought I had the experience and those two weeks working with tree cutters at 16 made me an expert! Well, I thought so. I sat there thinking, all I need is a ruddy big chainsaw. At that, I heard a car pulling up.

"Morning," came a voice from the car. Walking across the

car park was Andy.

"Hi Bud, I suppose you want a cuppa and some breakfast?"

"Mmm, you read my mind," he said as he walked up the garden.

An hour and a half later we were settling down on the bench with tea in one hand and bacon butty in the other hand.

"Don't tell Scarlett," I said to Andy. As we tucked into our food, I looked at the tree. "You don't happen to have a ruddy big chainsaw, Andy?"

"Yeh, why?"

"Really?" I said.

"It's in the back of the van, why?"

"I couldn't loan it off you for a couple of days, could I?"

"What're you doing with it?" he asked.

"I'm just going to chop some logs up." Well, I wasn't going to tell him what I really wanted it for. Andy, knowing me as he did, meant he probably would not loan it me. I thought I would show him. "Have faith in me, Andy."

Well, I'd show him what I had done after.

Andy left, handing me the chainsaw and some petrol. "Cheers – I will get it back to you in a couple of days."

"No hurry," he said as he climbed into his car and drove off.

I checked on Scarlett and the dogs. They were all fast asleep in the garden on the trampoline. I was about to head up the field when a brand new tractor pulled into the car park. Chris jumped out and walked over. "I suppose you want a cuppa?"

"Yes, please," came the reply, "and a sandwich if one's going."

Crickey, was I ever going to get on with attacking that tree? No explosives this time as I was going to use my head.

As we drank and ate my second sandwich of the day, I said, "Hey Chris, what's with the tractor? It looks new."

"It is new, I've just collected it."

"Looks expensive," I said.

"Yeh, cost me £45,000."

"Wow, looks a stunner."

Then an idea sprung. "Hey Chris, while you are here, how about helping me with a tree I want to bring down?"

"What're you thinking?"

"Well, once I've sawn it down, you could drag it out of the way for me with your new tractor."

"Sure, I can do that," Chris said.

"Great!" We headed up the field in his new tractor pulling up near to the tree. I climbed out of the cab and walked towards the tree.

"Where do you want me to park up?" Chris asked.

"Over there, to the right of the tree, as it'll come down to the left."

"You know what you're doing?" he asked.

"Yes, sure. I used to work for the forestry cutting trees down all the time." Well it was a little white lie, but close to the truth.

Chris got out of his cab and walked over to watch me. "I'm going to cut a cheese-like shape in the bottom of the tree, then start to cut it from behind and it wall fall that way, away from the gate and the tractor."

All was going well. I started to cut into the tree; the chainsaw was going through it like butter. I now started to cut the rest of the cheese-like shape into the tree. "Yeh, it's looking good," I said to Chris who was standing there with a concerned look on his face. "Don't worry it's going great guns."

I went to the back of the tree and started to saw through to the cheese shape. I stopped and said, "I just need to go a bit more and it will fall that way." Just as I started the chainsaw up and went for the final big cut, the wind suddenly picked up. The large tree rocked back on itself, snapping the chain on the saw. I just watched open-mouthed as it came backwards the other way. Oh crap, there was nothing I could do.

"Watch out, Chris," I shouted.

"Oh no no no, God no!" hc was shouting as the tree slammed through the middle of the tractor crushing it like a pancake.

'Oh hell', I thought, not saying anything. It's the first time I had seen Chris cry.

All he kept saying was, "Me tractor, me tractor, look at my tractor!"

I was trying my hardest not to laugh as I could see the funny side, but I knew if Chris saw me he would have given me a slap. The thought of that was just making things worse. I then said, "Chris, you are insured?"

"Yes!" he said, running towards me. I ran down the field

with him hot on my heels.

I was shouting, "Well, that's ok then!" And he was saying, "That's beside the point. You said you knew what you were doing!" He eventually ran out of breath.

"Now, let's have a cup of tea and address the situation."

"Tea? Tea!" he said. "Oh go on, then."

As we sat looking up the field at the mess drinking a cup of tea, I was thinking, (well I would not dare say it out loud) 'I've broke the chainsaw, destroyed my gate, fence and a bloody new tractor'. I could not stop myself, the words just came out. "How are we going to move the tree now, Chris?"

"Oh, sod off," he said and we both eventually had a laugh about it.

A few days later, the tractor had been collected and he was having another new one under insurance as I had completely destroyed the first one beyond repair. The fence was repaired by Andy, along with a new gate. I had his chainsaw fixed before he came as I did not want to tell him what I had done. But Chris turned up and said, "Has he told you how he broke your chainsaw?"

"Cheers, Chris," I said.

Just over a week later, Chris was told he could collect his

tractor. I thought I would surprise him by turning up with a bottle of champagne. I had this idea of smashing it against the side of the tractor to christen it as you would a ship as it sails its maiden voyage. I walked into the dealership where Chris was standing proudly next to his new tractor. I walked straight over and smashed the bottle of champagne against the tractor shouting, "I christen this tractor…" I never got to the end of what I was saying as instead of the bottle smashing, it bounced off the large tractor light and it was the light that smashed, not the bottle. "Oh crap," I said.

"Steve, what the f…." he said, as he chased me out of the dealership.

Chris does now have his new tractor which I am not allowed anywhere near, and yes, we are still friends.

A week later I was out moving some pigs into trailers. I had sold some for breeding to another farmer. As we finished loading them he said just before he drove off, "Did there used to be a tree there?"

"Yeh, there did," I said, as I walked away chuckling out loud thinking about it. I still reckon it wasn't my fault.

CHAPTER 13
SCARLETT GOES TO SCHOOL

We had been home about a week doing our normal day-to-day things. Alex going to school and me running the farm, feeding the animals, cleaning them out, dealing with any illnesses that the animals may have. I now injected the animals myself and administered any tablets to them as I had learnt this from the vets when they had been called out and if I could do it myself, then this would save a lot of money. We were selling a lot of the piglets to other farmers and we had also started Pig Days. They were like Red Letter Days, where people could become a pig farmer for the day. The cost was forty-five pounds for one person or seventy-five pounds for two. It was working well as I was getting twenty people every other Saturday coming to the farm. It was great fun and a very good earner. They would arrive in the morning for coffee and cake. I would give them some training about pigs in a fun way, then they would do a 'twenty questions' competition, which was all about pigs, of course. While they were doing this, I would bring Scarlett in from the other room to say hello, which they all loved. Then they would go outside to be with the pigs, which involved feeding them and mucking out. We also gave them fruit and vegetables, their favourite being grapes. I would of course find a piglet for them to hold which they all wanted to have a photo with. I never let them in with the boars as they could be a bit nasty, as I had learnt to my peril on a couple of occasions. We ended the day by going back into the farmhouse for sausage sandwiches. I know, a bit weird considering they had just been cuddling a piglet. While they were eating their sandwiches, Scarlett would be walking around watching them; if she only knew what they were eating, I'm sure she would not have been as nice as she was. So this was becoming our daily way of life until we had another two phone calls with weird requests!

We had a Korean National TV show phone us wanting to fly over a crew to film Scarlett and they would arrive next weekend. They asked if I could find somewhere for them to stay. I thought of my friend Ian who runs a place called The Old Hand & Diamond near Crew Green. It's a great pub, which does wonderful home cooked meals and a great place to stay over. Then we had a phone call from the BBC asking if they could come and film a show at our place called Be My Guest. I accepted, not knowing what it was. "Oh well, in for a penny, in for a pound," I thought, as they wanted to pay us, then who was I to say no.

Firstly, we had the arrival of the film crew from the Korean TV show. They arrived Friday afternoon after checking into The Old Hand & Diamond. There were four of them, the presenter and three others who dealt with the filming and sound. They wanted to film Scarlett bouncing on the trampoline and nothing else. I told them about Scarlett living in the house and having her own bedroom, how she was able to turn the TV on and change the channel, how she went down a slide and her dancing. We showed them all of this but, all they seemed interested in was Scarlett on the trampoline. Scarlett was getting bigger now as pigs do grow quite quickly so she was finding the trampoline more difficult as she grew larger. They got some film of her on the trampoline which wasn't her best performance and they also got a lot of film of Scarlett doing the other things as well as her dancing. "I am so sorry we did not get her bouncing as high as she used to go." I said, explaining now that she was bigger it made it hard to do. They also filmed her going down her new large slide, which put a smile on their faces.

I had bought the largest slide I could find, which was about ten feet high and it had a slide about thirty feet long. I had asked a local carpenter to build a long wooden walk way up to the slide which was high on both its sides, so Scarlett, when walking up would not get scared or fall off. When they came to install the ramp, they looked at me weirdly. "You want this ramp to help a pig go down a slide?" he asked.

"Yes, that's right," I said. He looked at me, and then at the slide, scratching his head, not knowing what to say, eventually he said, "Well you're the customer." Then he started to unload all the materials and tools to make the ramp with the help of his son. I kept seeing them talking and chuckling, I could only think it was about what I had asked them to do.

Three hours later, the ramp was assembled and it looked great. It was about eighteen feet long and came in two parts. The ramp had a pair of stilts underneath to support the frame as it was so heavy. I made them a cup of tea and said now is the time to see if Scarlett will go on it. We watched as Scarlett sniffed around the bottom of the ramp and started to walk slowly up towards the top sniffing all the time at all the new smells. We walked around to the front of the slide as Scarlett reached the top. We looked at each other wondering what Scarlett would do next as she was very high up and it was a long way down. Scarlett started to back up so I called her name. "Scarlett, come on!" I clapped my hands and repeated "Come on!" At that she walked forward, sat down and pushed herself off. She zipped along so fast, as she hit the bottom. The speed Scarlett was travelling meant she shot across the garden, rolling over. I was worried in case she had hurt herself, but she got up and ran to the ramp and spent the next hour playing on her new toy.

The carpenter just sat there laughing, "I have never seen anything like it." He took a few photos of her, I then paid him.

"Thanks for making the ramp, she loves it." He left chuckling to himself. I sat down to watch Scarlett playing on her slide. The dogs had come 'round from the other garden to see what all the fuss was about, they were sitting watching Scarlett and at no point did they attempt to go on the slide.

All this was what the TV crew from Korea were filming. It was their last day and it must have been the hottest day of the year. Alex was home from school and was in the large outdoor pool we had. An idea came to mind I knew Scarlett would not want to do much as it was so hot, so I pulled the slide nearer to the pool. Alex started to watch me shaking her head knowing what I had thought of. "You are joking Dad?"

"What?" I said, with a smile on my face. The film crew were watching, not knowing what I had in mind. The end of the slide was now at the pool edge. "Scarlett!" I called and she came out from the front door. She must have been sleeping, as she looked very sleepy and just plodded towards the bottom of the ramp not noticing I had moved the slide. The film crew had now got the gist of what I had done and had set themselves at the other side of the pool.

None of us could ever have guessed what happened next; Scarlett got to the top of the slide and sat down, pushed herself of as normal, and as she reached the pool she slid across the top of the water half the length of the pool before sinking. Scarlett then came to the surface and swam to the edge of the pool. Alex was in the pool clapping, so were the film crew.

"Wow! That was great. Did you get it on film?" I asked.

"Yes we got the lot, thanks." Alex was now walking to the ramp followed closely by Scarlett. Alex came down the slide, still followed closely by Scarlett, straight into the pool both laughing. It is hard to describe the noise when a pig laughs but if you ever hear a pig laugh, it is something you will never forget.

"That's a rap," said the TV host for the show, we have

more then we wanted. They thanked me shaking my hand and left with big smiles on their faces, waving all the time to Scarlett, as they left.

I sat in the garden with the two dogs for the next two hours just watching Alex and Scarlett play in the pool together. Alex was swimming around closely followed by Scarlett. Eventually they finished playing and got out of the pool. "Having fun Alex?" I asked. Alex was smiling, she had the best time. "Scarlett is so great, what a swimmer." I fed Alex, Scarlett and all the other animals on the farm. Feed time on the farm normally took me about an hour as long as it went smoothly.

The next morning when I took Alex to school, I was asked if I would go and see the head. She asked me if I would bring Scarlett in to visit the children and give a talk, which I agreed to do. Two days later I was on my way to school with Alex, towing Scarlett in her trailer. We pulled into the car park where everyone started to mill around the trailer to see what we had inside it. I parked up while Alex and the girls went to assembly. I was told they would come and get me after.

Thirty minutes later I was asked if I could go into the main hall where everyone was waiting for us. Scarlett walked into the main hall, wearing her lead and was met with loads of laughter and cheers which she loved. I stood at the front with her as the girls began to ask lots of questions about Scarlett. I told them about her and all the other pigs. I was trying to be as informative as possible. I hoped they would learn something from our visit, which by the end of my talk I think they all had. When I had finished they all gathered around to stroke her, which she loved. Scarlett seemed to love all the attention she got when out. I loaded her back up and decided to take her for a walk in the park in Shrewsbury. Scarlett walked great on the lead, just like a dog and would sit and wait at the side of the road and move only when told to.

As we entered the park I was mobbed by people who wanted their photo with Scarlett or just wanted to stroke her and find out why I was taking a woolly pig for a walk in the park. I think by some of the looks I was getting people were thinking who on earth is this crazy guy walking a pig. As we eventually got to the bottom of the park there was an ice cream van. We had two 99 ice creams with a chocolate flake in each. I gave one to Scarlett which she ate in seconds and I had the other. It was funny to see her eat it with everyone watching. She loved it and spent the next half hour licking her lips and we headed back to the trailer. I started to take her for a walk in the park on a regular basis and we became a feature, people heard about me and the pig and would come to the park on the off chance they might see us. I had a leather harness, handmade for her which Scarlett looked great in. Also more and more schools had heard about our visit to my daughter's school and wanted Scarlett to visit their schools, which we did.

We had also been asked to be in the Shrewsbury Town Carnival Float, which we had agreed to do. This entailed my daughter and Scarlett being in the back of a flatbed trailer, so everyone could see them and me towing them. Alex was dressed up as Nanny McPhee and Scarlett was dressed up as a pig. The day went well, with everyone waving at Scarlett and Alex. They both seemed to love the attention. By now we were doing more and more things around Shrewsbury. I also used to take Scarlett into the town centre for a walk, everyone would come out of the shops to see us and stroke Scarlett as they had never seen a woolly pig. Every spare minute Alex and I had was spent on taking the pig out. I had also noticed Alex had a way with animals, especially Scarlett. They got on really well and Scarlett seemed to follow Alex everywhere.

One afternoon Alex was down in the lower field riding her horse. Scarlett had gone down with her to watch. Alex had been down the field for about an hour when Scarlett appeared at the back door of the farm, running back and forth looking quite distressed. I looked out of the back door and could see Alex's horse walking around the field on its own. "Where's Alex?" I thought. I rushed down to the field to find Alex on the floor crying and rubbing her leg. "Are you all right, what happened?"

"The horse brushed up against the outside of the stable and knocked me off. Dad, how did you know I was in trouble?"

"Scarlett came up to the house and told me."

"You are a good girl," Alex said as she gave Scarlett a cuddle. Alex got to her feet and went back towards her horse.

"Do you need a hand getting back on?" I asked.

"No I'm fine thanks, but can you stay and watch?"

"Yes of course I can." I stayed with Alex while she rode for another hour. Afterwards, we settled all the horses down for the night and headed back to the house. Alex had bruised her leg badly but she would live to fight another day.

"What a clever pig Scarlett is." I said to Alex.

"Can I have her sleep in my room tonight, Dad?"

"Yes, no problem. Alex, shall I make you all something to eat and bring it up?"

"Yes sure, thanks Dad." Later on that evening I went up

to see where everyone was. Alex was fast asleep in bed, Scarlett and the two dogs were lying at the bottom of the bed all snuggled up together.

That evening it started to rain very heavily. We had put underground drainage pipes on the field where the pigs were. We had problems with drainage as the soil was mostly clay. We had a drainage ditch between the farmhouse and the field to prevent the garden and house from flooding. We had a cellar which I had tanked to stop it getting damp and fitted an underground drainage pump to keep the cellar dry and free from flooding. The pipe from the cellar ran into the drainage ditch.

On this evening the rain was getting heavier and heavier. It was about 1 am in the morning when I looked outside the back door to see a wall of water running down across the field which had completely overcome the drainage ditch and was flooding the patio and the garden. The pump from the cellar was now under water so I knew the cellar would flood if I did nothing about it. I went into Alex's room. "Alex, Alex, can you get up, the ditch is flooding."

"What?" Alex said.

"The ditch is flooding and the pump coming from the cellar is under water."

"What are we going to do, Dad?" Alex asked.

"I need to get into the ditch and I need you to hand me an extension pipe so I can fit it to the cellar pipe so we can drain the water off. We will have to have it going into the garden for now."

Alex put on her clothes and her wellies, while I just rushed out in my pyjamas without thinking. There was water everywhere; it looked like a river running down the field. Luckily the pig houses were on stilts so they were all safe. We just needed to protect the house from flooding. I had been down to the shed and found a long length of pipe which I knew would do the job. I just had to fit it to the pipe which was now below the water level in the ditch. The water in the ditch must have been about six feet deep. I had to throw big concrete blocks and anything else I could find to stand on. Alex had been down to check on the cellar which was starting to flood as the water had nowhere to go.

"Dad, the pump in the cellar is making horrible noises and water is coming up from the floor," Alex said as she came out of the house.

I was now starting to panic, which is nothing new, the rain was coming down even harder now. "Dad, what are we going to do and why have you thrown loads of wood into the ditch?"

"Mmmm, not sure to be honest, Alex I thought of standing on them."

"But they will sink, Dad."

"Yes I know, I did not think of that."

We were standing there getting wetter and wetter. "Dad, why are you still in your pyjamas?" Alex asked. Before I could answer, I heard a large noise coming from up the field.

"What was that?" Alex asked.

"I don't know," I said looking up the field. All of a sudden I realised what it was; at the far end of the field was another large drainage ditch which blocked now and again. It must have blocked and broke, and all I could see was a large amount of water coming towards us.

"Dad what are we going to do?" Alex looked really worried. Before I could think what I was doing, I had jumped into the drainage ditch. The water was freezing!

"Alex hand me that pipe, quickly," I shouted trying not to sound too panicky. I had to dive under the water to find the pipe coming from the cellar, the water was starting to spill over the sides, it was so cold. I eventually found the pipe and asked Alex to pass the other pipe to me. "Dad, the water is getting nearer."

"Ok, don't worry!" I said. I knew if I did not fit the extension pipe we would be in trouble and the house would be flooded. I was also trying to understand why the water was not draining away. My head was just above the water, I had one pipe in one hand and one in the other. I had one eye on what I was doing and one on the water coming towards us.

All of a sudden I felt the two pipes connect, "Alex take the end of the pipe over to the high part of the garden."

"Dad get out of there, the water is coming!" I knew I had to have a quick look at the main drain pipe which drained water off to the main sewer pipe. I dived under the water to where the pipe was and felt a big stone blocking it. I came to the surface.

"Come on Dad, get out." Alex cried.

"Just a minute," I said before diving back under the water. I grabbed the stone and with one big heave I came to the surface throwing the stone out of the gully. I scrambled out of the ditch just as a wall of water hit it. I ran towards Alex who was standing on the higher part of the garden.

The garden and the ditch sloped off to the right which was great, as all the water just ran off to the bottom end of the garden and car park. The garden and car park flooded in seconds. "I just hope this extension pipe works." Just as I said that, the water started to gush out of the pipe. We both jumped for joy. I looked through the cellar window and could see the water that had started to come in was going down.

"Dad!" Alex shouted. "Look at the ditch, the water is going down." I turned to look and Alex was right, the water was starting to recede.

"Phew," I thought as the disaster was averted. "This is not normal." We went back inside, both of us soaking wet and cold. I ran a bath, as I was freezing. Alex made a hot chocolate drink and took it off to bed with her.

"Night Alex, thanks for your help," I shouted as I climbed into the bath with a big mug of tea.

"Night, Dad," she replied. I lay in the bath thinking about the evening's events and had a good chuckle. I just hoped all was ok with the animals. "Well, all will become clear in the morning."

The next morning I looked outside the window and the whole place was a mess. There was mud all over the garden and the fencing was down all around the garden. The water had gone from the car park and garden, just the odd big puddle here and there. The horse paddock was still under water, so I would keep them in the stables for the day and exercise them on the road around the farm. Thank God I had spent the money putting the road in last year, as it was completely dry. I went outside with tea in hand, leaving Alex fast asleep in bed, as it was not a school day.

I let the horses out onto the road and I gave them some feed, before heading over to check on the pigs and llamas. As I walked towards the pig area I could see the donkeys in the top paddock eating grass without a care in the world. "They are all right," I thought. As I went through the gate I was met by the llamas running towards me.

"Morning!" I shouted, as they got nearer. I went into the feed shed where I used to keep the pig feed before we had the five ton feed tower installed.

We kept the fruit and veg in here to feed the pigs and the llamas. I gave the llamas a bucket full of apples and carrots which they started to eat as soon as the buckets hit the floor. I started to walk to the pig pens with my heart in my mouth not knowing what I would find. Only a few hours ago the whole field had been under water. The pig pens were very quiet and muddy with large puddles of water; luckily the decking we had fitted a few months ago was still in place. As I rattled the buckets, pigs ran out from everywhere, they were all fine. Wow! I could not believe they had all survived the storm.

Alex came running out of the house shouting, "Dad, Dad!"

As I saw her I said, "Don't worry, Alex, they are all ok. The decking has worked."

"Dad, no, have you checked on the badgers?"

At the far end of the fields next to the Christmas trees was a badger set. This is where a large group of badgers live under the ground. There were large badger holes in the ground along the hedgerow. Alex and I had seen several badgers playing around there early spring. We used to take a flask of tea and something to eat some evenings waiting to watch them come out. Badgers become very active late evenings, being most active at night. We either were there late in the day or early morning as the sun came up. There was a large area that flooded by the hedgerow as it was at the bottom of the field. The Christmas trees were on a bank where all the rain water would drain down to the bottom of the field.

"Oh heck, Alex, I'd not thought of that." We grabbed our wellies and started to walk up the field. It was hard going as the ground was very wet. I had a spade to hand, not sure what I was going to do with it. As we got nearer to the top corner of the field we could see it was completely flooded. There was now a large lake at the bottom of the field which was covering the hedge.

"Oh no, Alex, the water has flooded the badgers' home."

We both stood looking at the water and then Alex said in a whisper, "Dad over there, look." In the far corner, huddled up under some tress was a large group of animals looking very distressed. "Dad, it's the badgers, we need to help them."

As we walked towards the water, keeping close to the Christmas trees as this area was the driest, I was thinking to myself, "What could we do to help them?" As we walked past the trees I was deep in thought.

"Dad?"

"Yes, Alex?"

"What's that noise?"

We stopped walking to listen. There was a thundering noise under the ground not far from the water's edge. We walked around trying to find where the noise was loudest. Alex had found something.

"Over here," she said.

As I walked closer, I could see a small whole in the ground

about 8 inches wide, where all the water draining off the field was going. "Alex, it's an underground drain. Well done finding it."

At that, an idea sprung to mind; if I dug a long channel in the ground from the hole to the large lake, it would start to drain. So, I got to work. As I dug, the hole began to get bigger and as I was digging, the ground either side was just falling back in as it was so wet. I stopped digging and turned to Alex who was now crying.

"We are not going to be able to save them, are we Dad?" Alex said.

I looked over at the badgers then back to Alex. "We will find a way, Alex," I said.

Then I heard a tractor in the next field. As I looked up, I saw Chris heading towards me with a big smile on his face. Chris was one of my farming neighbours, a great guy who had helped me before by giving me a lot of useful advice. A very likeable guy with a cheeky side to him.

"Dad, it's Chris." Alex ran towards the tractor waving at Chris. He slowed down and Alex climbed up into the tractor. I could see her telling Chris all about what was happening, pointing at the badgers. I was now wondering if he was going to help, as I knew a lot of farmers don't like badgers as they can spread a disease to their cattle. We'll leave the arguments on either side of that debate there.

Chris started on his way towards me with Alex next to him. "Morning Steve, looks like you need some help."

"That would be great, Chris, what do you have in mind?"

Without even answering me, he started to dig by the drain hole. Before long, Chris had dug a trench a metre wide into the lake. Wow! The water started to flow really fast through the trench and down the hole. Chris and Alex got off the tractor and walked over.

"Yeh Dad, the water is going down!"

I looked and the water was receding. "Thanks Chris, you're a star."

"No worries," he replied. Chris then explained that the hole was a natural drain and was very deep. "When the lake has gone down far enough, I will dig a channel all the way around it using the soil to build a bank," he explained.

"That's great. That will create a natural defence to protect the badger set. Fancy a bacon sandwich and tea, Chris?"

"Now you're talking," he said. Alex and I walked back to the house to make the food and tea leaving Chris digging in his tractor.

It was turning into a really hot day. The ground was drying out fast. An hour later we were walking back to Chris with his bacon sandwich and tea. We had eaten ours as we were both starving. As we got nearer, we could not believe how much he had done. Most of the water had gone just leaving the field in a muddy mess. He had dug a trench and built a bank all the way 'round the lake. Plus, he had dug a meter-deep trench from it to the drain hole. He said it should never happen again. It would just turn into a small pond and watering hole for the animals and our sheep.

As Chris devoured his sandwich and slurped his tea we noticed the badgers basking in the sun. "Well, they all seem to be happy," Chris said as he left in his tractor.

"Cheers, Chris!" we both said, waving goodbye as he left. Later that day, Alex and I walked back up to where the drama had started that morning. We could see the badgers playing by their home; you could see they had been digging around them clearing the mess up. With a smile on my face I looked at Alex saying in a self-assured way, "Well, that's another disaster I diverted."

"You mean Chris did," said Alex as she walked away chuckling to herself.

CHAPTER 14
BBC COME TO FILM

A few weeks later it was time for the BBC film crew to arrive; they were coming to film a new TV show. I had to turn my house into a guest house for the week. I would have a different guest to stay every day. I think they wanted us to do the show because of my pig Scarlett! I am famous because of my pig. What an accolade. The new show was called 'Be My Guest'.

They were going to start filming a week before the guests started to arrive. They were going to film Alex and me getting the farm-house ready for the guests. They arrived early on Monday morning. Nadia Sawalha's husband was going to direct the show, (for the life of me, I cannot remember his name), he was also doing the filming. They had a soundman and a runner whose job was to get everything they wanted and deal with any problems. I was going to have to do most of the work, as Alex would be at school during the day.

We sat round the kitchen table after Alex had gone to school and I started to plan what I was going to do. I was going to strip the bed first which would be easy as I was used to doing the laundry. I was going to sleep in the spare room as the guest could have the main bedroom which had an en suite bathroom. The bedding was stripped and put into the washing machine. They were following me everywhere with the camera filming my every move. The washing machine was on and I was going to put tea and coffee making facilities in the bedroom. I had to clean the bathrooms, hoover and dust everywhere.

I could hear the washing machine finish and I shouted downstairs to the runner and asked if she could open the washing machine. "Err Steve, can you come here and look at the washing?" I went downstairs and on walking into the utility room I said, "Oh, no! It's green, I can't believe it." I started to have a good rant, not noticing that they were filming me having it. The cream quilt and pillows were now green, along with the fitted sheets, I could not believe it. "Don't worry," I said. "I will get a new set when I go for the food this afternoon." The rest of the day was pretty uneventful.

I went to get Alex from school and left the film crew back at the house. "Hi Dad, how is it all going?" Alex said.

"Well it was going ok, until I dyed the bedding green."

"Oh no, Dad what are you like!"

"We can get a new set when we go for the food," I replied. On arriving home, the film crew were waiting in the car park for me so they could film us. They filmed us going up to the house. Alex asked, "Can I go and play in the garden?"

"Yes, of course," I said. Off she shot, leaving me with all the bags of shopping on the front doorstep.

"Thanks Alex."

"No worries! Dad," came the reply. I went straight upstairs leaving the bags of shopping on the doorstep. I decided making the bed first, would be a good idea. About twenty minutes later, I heard Alex screaming. "Scarlett! No!" I ran downstairs, followed by the film crew and there on the doorstep was Scarlett and the food shop was everywhere. Scarlett was covered in baking powder.

The shopping was ruined. "Alex, how did she get out of the garden?"

Alex shrugged her shoulders. "I don't know."

"Did you leave the gate open?"

"No!" she said, very sheepishly. I was about to shout at Alex, when my eyes were drawn towards Scarlett. Now the dogs had joined her, and all three of them were eating the eggs. We all started to laugh. "I need a beer!" I said, walking off into the kitchen leaving everyone on the doorstep.

The next day I went back to Tesco's for more food, making sure Scarlett got nowhere near it when I got back. The rest of the week was pretty uneventful and by Thursday evening everything was ready. The house was all clean and tidy, food was in the cupboards, I had baked a fruit cake, and Alex had baked some cupcakes. Every evening Alex was helping me clean the house and I had made a sign for the door. Everything was ready for our first guest. Well, that is what I thought.

I sat back and relaxed as the film crew left; it was now quite late on a Thursday evening and the first guest was arriving around 10 am next day. There was supposed to be one guest staying each day, then leaving the following morning. I sat up till about 1 am with Scarlett and the dogs.

Scarlett by now was very well trained and she could pick the TV remote up and change the channel over, Scarlett even had her favourite TV shows. She also barked like a dog as she thought she was one; living with the dogs had worn off I think. Scarlett would knock on the door if she wanted to go out and would take herself off to her bed when tired. Scarlett was starting to get bigger; there would come a time when she would be too big to live in the house but I was not going to think about that yet and just enjoy what we all had together.

We were both up early the next morning to make sure all was ready. The front room had been turned into a guest sitting room. I was going to have another go at cleaning the chimney but remembered what happened last time, so I decided, best not. The main bedroom upstairs which had an en-suite was all ready with tea and coffee making facilities and whatever else you would expect in a hotel.

The camera crew had been with us an hour and I heard them say, "He is here." They went outside to film the guest arriving. I heard a knock at the door. I went to answer it and was met by a guy who was about six feet tall. He was larger than life.

"Morning, how are you?" I said. "Welcome to Ayredale Farm."

"Morning," he answered. I showed him into the front room and went to fetch him some tea and cake. In the afternoon, the film crew had arranged an activity for the guest to do. Apparently he liked kick-boxing, so they had arranged an afternoon of training and fighting in a boxing ring.

I was to go with him and the film crew came along to film what the guest, whose name was John, was going to do. It was a hot day, the film crew had asked me to wear gym wear and trainers. I should have known what they were up to.

We arrived in my car and had a good talk on the way over; John was from London and he was a train driver on the underground. We walked over to the gym and I could see the Film Producer talking to the gym owner. Not knowing what was going to happen next, I walked with John into the gym. He had a couple of others in the gym, to work out with him. I was leaning against the wall minding my own business, when they called me over to join in the work out. I thought nothing of it as we were running on the spot and doing other warm-up exercises.

It was when John and I were asked into the ring and they started to pad us up and I was given a head guard, I knew then I had been had. I watched from the side as John worked out with a small chap. John was very good at kick-boxing and he held his own. It was now my turn, the chap John had been sparring with left the ring and out of the corner of my eye, I saw a woman walking to the ring. "Oh, this is all right." I thought. "No problem here!" I held the ring rope up, as she climbed into the ring and I cheekily said to her, "I will go easy on you."

We stood opposite each other and as I heard the word fight, I was hit across the head before I even knew what was happening. Then it happened, I got a good beating, even when I decided right, lady or no lady, you are in for it now, I still did not get a hit in. I was kicked and punched all over the ring. Thank God for the protective padding. When it had finished, I was lying on the ring floor, the girl came up to me and said, "Thanks for going easy on me."

In the background I could hear the film crew saying, "Wow! That will make great footage."

"Yeah, cheers," I said. They all walked out of the gym laughing. John helped me to my feet laughing.

"I have to say that was funny, Steve!"

"Cheers, John" I said, laughing, happy that I had amused everyone.

We drove back to the farm and cooked dinner. We had a great evening. John ended the evening tucked up on the settee with his arm around Scarlett. We got on really well and we could relax now the film crew had gone. We had a couple more beers and headed off to bed. "Night, John!"

"Night, Steve!" was his reply.

The next morning, I was up early getting Alex her breakfast and laying out cereals for John in the front room. I had made a menu so he could choose what he wanted to eat. The camera crew arrived and were talking to John in the front room. John had chosen a full English breakfast and I was busy cooking it when he walked into the kitchen, followed by the film crew.

"Steve?" John said. "As I am having such a great time, I would like to stay another night, is that all right?" Alex looked up at me from the breakfast table with a look of horror on her face.

"Err, hmm, that should be okay," I said, "no problem."

"Thanks," John said and he turned to go back into the front room. I turned to the camera crew. "Oh, crap," I said. "Where do I put the other guest who is arriving in a short while?"

After John had finished breakfast he went for a walk outside. I cleared everything away and turned to Alex. "Can you help me set the other room up?"

"Yeah sure Dad, no problem," she replied. We rushed upstairs and prepared the spare room and two hours later the room was ready, well, I thought it was.

John was in his room watching TV when the next guest arrived. I opened the door and was met by a lady wearing Victorian clothes, "Wow!" I thought, "that's different." I welcomed her into the lounge and offered her refreshments, which went down well. Her name was Lucy, she seemed to be very fussy and I was starting to realise this was going to be a long day. After Lucy finished her drink and cake she asked me if she could freshen up before going out for the afternoon.

I showed Lucy her room and that is when it started. She found cobwebs in places that you would never look. The towels were not fluffy enough, the soap was the wrong kind, the en-suite was not big enough and so the list went on. I was sure the film crew were telling the guests to be as awkward as possible.

We were going out in the afternoon and John was going to stay in his room. I was asked to take Lucy to a Victorian farm. "This is weird!" I thought, taking someone who lives this way every day, to a place where they also lived and wore the same clothes. "Freaky!" I thought.

We arrived at the Victorian farm about forty minutes later. The film crew were already waiting for us. I left them to it while they went around the farm, filming Lucy. I did not want to get roped into anything else. It was about two hours later when they came back to the car that we set off, back to the farm. When we got back Lucy went to her room to freshen up for dinner, she appeared a few times to moan about this and that I was starting to just nod and not really listen to what she was complaining about.

It was lucky that a good friend of mine had come over a few hours earlier to help cook dinner which was ready to serve an hour later. John ate his dinner in the front room whilst Lucy ate her dinner in her room, fussy sod; she was getting to me, with all her quirky ways and all her asks. I had to count to ten every time she called for me.

Thank God it was now morning and they had both had breakfast and were now leaving. I bid them a safe journey and thanked them for coming. I had two more days of this, as I had another guest arriving in an hour who turned out to be two female friends and the following day we had a single lady to stay. All went well over the following two days with the guests. Secretly, one of the guests was a Hotel Inspector and was going to judge us and then the following week she was going to another house to do the same. "I wonder who the Hotel Inspector was," I asked Alex, after the last guest had left. "I bet it was that Victorian woman," she replied.

Well, it was a couple of weeks later when they came to film us getting the results of the contest and which house had won. You are wondering what happened next? Ok, I will tell you. They filmed at the other location where they had also turned their home into a B&B for a week. When they took the show to the BBC to air, Channel 4 had just started airing a show called Be My Guest. They had beaten the BBC to it and the BBC were reluctant to air another similar show. It is now in the archives of the BBC maybe to be aired one day.

A couple of weeks later, when life had gone back to normal. Alex was going to school and I was busy on the farm with the pigs. I was now supplying farms all over the county which was keeping me very busy. All the animals were doing well on the farm and things could not be better. I was now planning a trip to London with Scarlett, but I could never have known how that day was going to be so weird.

CHAPTER 15
NO 10 & BUCKINGHAM PALACE

All had gone back to normal and I was sitting at home on a
Sunday afternoon after saying goodbye to all the people who
had spent the day on the farm with the pigs. As they left with
boxes of pork under their arms, I looked at Scarlett and the
dogs, who were all curled up together under the large willow
tree in our garden. Alex had gone for a walk down to the
field, closely followed by the two farm cats, llamas, her horse
and the donkeys, it was an odd sight but it put a smile on my
face. "Ruby, where is Alex going?" I said to her. At that,
Ruby looked up and she shot across the garden and down the
field after her. Cerys just lifted her head, before settling back
down with Scarlett. "This is not a bad life," I thought, but I
felt an urge inside me telling me it was too quiet and I had to
do something. That's when the idea popped into my head,

instead of taking Scarlett for her Monday walk around the park in Shrewsbury, I would hitch the trailer up and take her for a walk around London. I started to get excited at the thought. It was about an hour later when Alex appeared, walking back towards the house with all the animals in tow. As Alex got nearer, I shouted to her, "I am taking Scarlett on a walk tomorrow!"

"What! Around the park?" came the reply.

"Err, not quite, I am taking her for a walk around London!"

"What! You are joking?" Alex said, as she looked closely at me. "Oh my God, I can tell you're not." Alex walked away towards the house giggling away to herself, shaking her head. "That's my dad!" I could hear her say, before she entered the house.

It was now Monday morning, I had hitched the trailer up and Scarlett was already harnessed up and waiting to go. Scarlett got very excited when I put the harness on her as she knew we were going somewhere. I had arranged for a friend to walk the dogs. Alex was going to a friend's after school and my friend would also see to all the other animals on the farm; everything was covered, nothing to worry about we could just enjoy our day out.

I dropped Alex off at school and Scarlett and I headed down the motorway. "Which route shall we take?" I said to myself, "The M1, or the M40? Mmm, I know, we'll take the M1." I knew that route into London better. I had set the satellite navigation up for a car park in Leicester Square, to which I had already phoned ahead and booked two spaces for the car and trailer. When I had told the car park attendant what I was doing, all I got was, "Yeah right!"

The traffic heading down was very busy and at a stand-still in places. When I saw a sign for a service station ahead, I decided to pull in and let Scarlett stretch her legs, also I could give her some water. We pulled in by the lorry-park; I leaned over the tail gate attaching the lead before opening the back down. Scarlett came out and we started to walk to a grassy area. "Wow! What's that?" I could hear and before long there was a throng of people around me, taking photos and stroking Scarlett. Scarlett loved all the attention she was getting and lapped it up.

"What are you doing here with a pig?" was the question.

"I am taking Scarlett for a walk around London." They all looked at me with a quizzical look on their faces.

"Why?" was the next question.

"Erhhh... I don't really know, it just felt like a good idea at the time." At that, I said my goodbyes and headed back to the trailer. Scarlett did not really want to go as she was enjoying all the attention. I loaded Scarlett back into the trailer and we headed off. It was about two hours later when we pulled into the car park in Leicester Square.

The attendant came over and I explained who I was, "You are the guy with the pig, is it in the back?" he asked.

"Yes she is!" At that he walked to the back. "Oh my God," I heard him say as he looked into the trailer. "It's woolly, like a sheep!"

"Yes, I call her a shig," I said, laughing but he did not laugh, just looked at me, like I was an idiot, or something.

"Why have you brought a pig to London?"

"I just fancied taking her for a walk," I replied. "Where are you from?" he asked.

"The other side of Birmingham, a place called Shrewsbury."

"So why have you come all this way?"

"I don't know really, just seemed a good idea." He showed me where to park and walked away shaking his head. Mmmm… I could see a pattern forming here, of what the main question would be asked of me all day.

I parked up and unloaded Scarlett. I had a rucksack which I loaded up with bottles of water, a dog's bowl, some food for Scarlett and nappy bags to pick up any poos Scarlett did along the way. "Well, are you ready Scarlett?" I said. She just looked up at me with excitement in her eyes. I took a deep breath and we headed out of the underground car park to appear on a side street, just off Leicester Square.

I started to walk down the street and noticed an old-fashioned barbers to my right. As we walked past the open shop door I heard, "What on earth is that?" A man came running to the door.

"Hi!" I said. "This is Scarlett and I am Steve."

"You just have to come into my shop," he said.

"Scarlett needs a haircut."

"Why have you brought a sheep to London?" he asked.

"It's not a sheep, it's a pig," I replied.

"No, way," he said. Everyone in the shop came for a closer look and Scarlett was enjoying the attention. "Do you think we could get Scarlett into the barber's chair for a trim, it will make a lovely photo?" he said.

"Well we can give it a try," I said. At that, the barber winched the chair down, I picked Scarlett up very carefully as pigs do not like being picked up as they have very sensitive bellies (that is why pigs squeal when you pick them up).

Scarlett was used to me handling her and I think she trusted me now. I slowly sat her on the chair as the barber winched her up. When she was at the correct height, the barber proceeded to give her a trim, which Scarlett did not seem to mind. By now there was quite a crowd outside the shop watching what was going on. Everyone had either cameras out or their phones taking photos. After about fifteen minutes we decided to leave. Scarlett jumped off the chair, we said our goodbyes and left the shop heading towards Nelson's Column with everyone waving and laughing as we left.

As we approached the Column I could see loads of people gathered around it. I wanted to walk across and head down towards The Houses of Parliament, as I knew there was a green across from it. As I got nearer to the Column, people started to run towards me and before long we could hardly move. We had tourists all around us taking photos and asking me her name and why I was in London. I was even asked if I was protesting against something. "No I am not," I told them, "I just wanted to walk my pig." God, I sound like Forrest Gump, I thought to myself.

We finally managed to get across Leicester Square, which

must have taken us half an hour at least. We started to head off down the road to Parliament. I noticed that when someone was walking towards us they would take a quick glance then a few seconds later they would stop in their tracks and you could hear them say, "It's a pig." I had started to count how many times this kept happening but gave up in the end as it was getting ridiculous how many times I heard them say, "It's a pig," and "Why are you in London with a pig?"

We finally got to the road opposite Parliament. While waiting for the lights to turn green, so we could cross over safely, Scarlett was sitting as she had been trained to when crossing a road. As we crossed, I noticed standing on the other side of the road a man I recognised. As I got nearer I thought to myself, that's Boris Johnson. As we reached his side of the road he was laughing and he said, "Why are you walking a pig in London?"

"I have been asked that all day, Boris," I said. "I just wanted to walk my pig," I said laughing.

"You really are out there!" Boris said.

"Funny you are not the first to say that," was my reply.

"Come on!" Boris said. "You follow me, we must get this pig into Parliament and I am sure there is a bridge in London, that if a pig walks over it, they say the Monarchy will fall, mmm. I better not," he said, laughing.

As we approached the Police Guards at Parliament, Boris said to them, "Don't worry, they are both with me."

"Are you sure?" said the policeman on the gate.

"Yes, yes, it's fine," Boris said. We were walking into the main communal area and a throng of people gathered 'round us, which was becoming quite the norm. Then I heard Boris say, "Oh I have an idea, follow me." We went through an area which seemed to be just for MPs and the odd visitor, which was funny, as we had both been given visitor badges.

"Come on you two, no time to waste," he said as we walked through another area and down a long corridor. A few other MPs had joined us, as they seemed to know what Boris may be up to. We went through a large door which I seemed to recognise and we were slap bang in the middle of the debating chamber. I could see the Speaker's Chair and the benches either side. "Come on," Boris shouted, "before we get caught."

"What?" I said.

"Come on, up here," as he gestured me towards the Speaker's chair.

"What, you want me to put Scarlett on the chair?" I asked, not believing what Boris was asking.

"Yes, yes," he said.

I laughed, "Boris you are as mad as me." We both laughed as I put Scarlett on the Speaker's chair. "And you said, I was out there, Boris," I said. He just kept laughing like a naughty school boy. We heard another door opening.

"Come on quick," he said, "Follow me before we get caught." All three of us ran off through a back door, even Scarlett seemed to be laughing.

We started to walk back to the main area and I could see a lot of security and an official looking man, on a phone. "We are in trouble here," I thought.

As we got nearer, the man asked, "Where are you going next?"

"Well I am walking back to Leicester Square."

Smashing! You are going right past Number 10 Downing Street aren't you?"

"Erhhh, yes I am," I replied.

"Well, would you be able to pop in and see Mr Cameron at Number 10, as he would like to meet your pig?"

"Ha ha ha, you are joking!" But as I said that, I could tell he was deadly serious.

"No I am not, can you attend?"

"Erhhh, yes, of course we can."

"Brilliant, yes he will be right over Prime Minister."

"What! That was him on the phone?" I asked.

"Yes it was and he will tell his staff to expect you. How long will it take for you to walk there?"

"About thirty minutes," I said.

"Superb, I will tell them you are on your way."

We left Parliament and started to walk towards Number 10. I was trying to comprehend what was going on and what had just happened. It just wasn't sinking in. I sat down on the grass outside Parliament for a few minutes, while I gave Scarlett some water, then she had a poo and a tinkle. I was glad Scarlett had waited to do that outside Parliament. "Right Scarlett, we had better go, don't want to be late for the Prime Minister." God that even sounded weird. Best foot forward and off we went. Thirty minutes later we were approaching the Police Guards outside Number 10.

"Ah!" A policeman said, "you must be Scarlett." Looking downwards and then addressing me, "You must be Mr Howell?"

"Guilty as charged," I said. The policeman just looked at me and said, "Why are you walking a pig around London?" I just shrugged my shoulders.

"Follow me then." We walked through the gates and up to the door. "Oh my God, are we really going into Number 10." I thought. The door opened and we were gestured inside.

"Please follow me," a young lady said, as we walked through into the back garden. "Would you like some tea and sandwiches?"

"Oh, yes that would be lovely thank you," I said.

As the young lady walked back into the garden with the refreshments, she was closely followed by Mr Cameron. "Good afternoon," he said.

"Afternoon sir, and call me Steve," I said.

"Please sit down, Steve." I sat down as Mr Cameron walked towards Scarlett, who was now flat out on the lawn. As Mr Cameron stroked Scarlett he said, "So why are you walking a pig around London?"

"Funny," I said. "Not been asked that today," I was laughing. "I just fancied taking her for a walk and we ended up here." We were there for about half an hour. We ate our sandwiches and drank our tea. Then we spent the rest of the time talking about farming in general and what his thoughts on it were; he seemed to have a passion for the countryside I remember thinking. I could see people hanging around in the background waiting for Mr Cameron. I stood up and said, "We must go, as we have a long drive back and thank you for having us."

"No, thank you, it has been interesting meeting you, and it's not every day you meet a woolly pig in London." I stirred Scarlett and we said our goodbyes. As I walked through the door of Number 10, I turned to wave goodbye.

"Surreal or what?" I was thinking. We carried on walking towards Nelson's Column and a weird thought sprung to mind. "Well, I have been in Parliament and been to Number 10, mmm; let's see if I can get into Buckingham Palace!"

As we approached Nelson's Column I could see the road down to Buckingham Palace. I did not know how I was going to do it, but I would think of something. As we walked down the road and Buckingham Palace got nearer I just kept thinking, well we got into Parliament and Number 10, so why not Buckingham Palace. It just all made sense to me.

Scarlett was getting tired so I walked her into the park, where I fed and watered her. She then settled down for a nap. While Scarlett was sleeping I was mulling over the day's events and a wry smile came over my face. I was not hungry as I had had some sandwiches at Number 10. "Why do they cut the crusts off sandwiches and what is it with a cucumber sandwich, I never quite got that one." I sat there thinking of how I was going to get inside Buckingham Palace, the thought never entered my head of 'don't be so stupid' and 'why are you thinking of getting Scarlett inside'. It was not the normal everyday thoughts. I just sat looking at the palace gates in the distance and thought,"How am I going to get past those guards?"

Scarlett started to stir. I looked at my watch, "Wow!" Two hours had gone by and it was now late afternoon. Scarlett got to her feet and I could tell she had a lot of energy. We started to walk through the park and made our way to the back wall of the Palace. As I was walking along the wall, I noticed two men coming towards me carrying a large box.

When they got nearer, the same question came, "Why are you walking a pig in London?" I was about to answer when an idea came to mind and before I could stop myself I asked the two men if they could put the box down for a minute by the wall. They looked at me and asked why.

"I will give you twenty pounds if you do!" I said. With no other questions, they put the box against the wall, and as I climbed on top of the box, they held Scarlett's lead.

"Here's the twenty pounds, can you pass me Scarlett?" I

said. "Be careful of her stomach." They picked her up carefully and passed Scarlett to me. I took off her lead and handed it over to one of the men.

"What are you going to do?" he asked, as I gave him the lead. Before I had time to answer, I lobbed Scarlett over the wall. "Wow!" one of the guys said. "I did not see that coming, you're crazy you are really out there, man." I heard Scarlett land and run off making her oink, oink sound. "Pigs are like cats and they know how to land as when they are piglets, their mother would toss them around if they got in the way of her food, that is why I knew she would be ok, going over and landing," I explained to the two men.

They both looked at me as if I were a nutter. "But why throw her over in the first place?" the one man asked.

"Erhhh! It just seemed like a good idea at the time."

"How are you going to get her back?" they asked me.

"Not thought of that one," I said.

They grabbed the box, "You never saw us and we never saw you," was their leaving shot. As they walked away I could hear them laughing. "What a plonker!" were the last words I heard them say.

How was I going to get Scarlett out? I said to myself. I know, I would just go up to the front gate and ask for her.

As I approached the main gate, I could see one of the guards. "Excuse me!" I said showing him her lead; my pig got off the lead and has gotten into the gardens at the back. The guard just looked at me as if I was a complete loony.

"Please sir, get away from the gate," was the reply.

"No really, you do not understand, I need to get my pig, I can't leave her," I said.

"Please sir, if you do not move away you will be arrested," he replied.

"I'm not going anywhere till I get my pig," I demanded.

At that, I could see another two guards coming over and what looked like a security guard. As they approached, the security guard said, "What seems to be the problem?"

"Look, my pig has got into the gardens at the back, and it will make one hell of a mess in the gardens, so I need to get it back." The look on their faces was that of amazement. I wish I had taken a photo.

He was just about to say something when he put his hand to his ear and then talked on a walkie- talkie, I think that's what you call them. "He's not joking; there is a pig in the garden and it's digging up the roses." They were all about to run off, so I shouted. "You will never catch her, I can get her."

They all looked at each other. "Look if you don't let me in, she will make a right mess."

"Ok! Check him over; leave your rucksack there," they said. After checking it and me over, I followed them around to the back of the palace, with just the lead in my hand, leaving everything else with the guard at the gate.

By now I had about twenty men with me, all in their regalia, you know their tall black furry hats and fully armed up. "You are not going to shoot her!" I said with a nervous laugh.

"No! Of course not, but we may shoot you," he said, laughing.

They all started to run around the garden after the pig, but to no avail. Even when they thought they had cornered her, Scarlett ran through their legs. All the time this was going on, I was standing between two guards. I felt like I was under house arrest. "I wish I had my camera," I said. "It would make a brilliant photo."

One of the guards chuckled. "You are lucky no one is at home, as this could have been even more serious."

About thirty minutes had gone by and they still had not caught Scarlett. I thought, "It's about time to go home." I turned to the one guard and said. "I think Scarlett has had enough fun now, I think I will take her home." At that I turned and called Scarlett. "Scarlett!" She started to run towards me. She came to my feet and I put her lead on.

They all just looked at me. "Could you have done that at any time?" one of the guards asked.

"Erhhh! Yes, sorry," I said, with a sheepish grin on my face.

One by one they all started to laugh. "You little sod." Some other harsher words were said. We walked back to the gate laughing. I was talking with them about my time in the armed forces and how I knew soldiers like a good joke.

By the time we had got back to the gate, we were all on first name terms. We all had a good chuckle about it. I also told them about the day's events and that I just had to bring Scarlett to the palace. We shook hands and said our goodbyes. I wished them well and said, "Stay safe out there and watch out for flying pigs."

"Sod off!" I heard one of them say, as I walked away chuckling to myself. As we walked back up the road, I could not believe what had gone on. What a day! Scarlett was none the worse for her ordeal and she seemed to like running around the garden, with everyone chasing her, just like the games we played back on the farm.

As we got to Nelson's Column I decided to walk through Leicester Square on the way to the car park. As we did so, I was looking at all the different films that were coming up for release and I noticed Nanny McPhee and the Big Bang was going to be released in a few months. "Mmmm," another, idea had sprung to mind. I was thinking, "Would Emma Thompson be interested in having Scarlett at the open evening of the film? That would look cool, Emma Thompson walking down the red carpet with Scarlett."

With that idea firmly stuck in my head, Scarlett and I headed towards the car park. I loaded Scarlett into the trailer; it was now 6 pm. I gave Scarlett some water and food. She ate, drank, and fell fast asleep. I was starving by now. All I'd had was a sandwich at Number 10, and a chocolate bar for breakfast. As we left, I waved to the parking attendant and we headed out of London. I saw a McDonalds on the way out, so I called in to the drive-through. I had two hamburgers and a McChicken sandwich, fries and coke. We hit the M1 about an hour later and headed home without stopping.

When we arrived home it was about 11 pm. I was so tired, I pulled into the car park and unloaded Scarlett. I think she had slept all the way home. We walked into the house and had a great welcome from the dogs. They were sniffing

Scarlett all over. "Must be loads of new smells on her," I thought. Alex was staying at her friend's house and I would collect her from school the next day. I made myself a drink and settled down on the sofa while the dogs and Scarlett were playing outside in the back garden.

It was now 12 am, I was sitting watching TV with my second cup of coffee, the dogs and Scarlett were all curled up on the rug by me. I began to chuckle as I thought about the day's events. Next morning I unloaded and cleaned the trailer out, the day went back to normality, as I fed all the animals and took bookings for our farm days. I also dealt with the sale of some pigs and the other jobs related to the farm. It was now time to get Alex. I picked her up and her first words were, "Well, how did it go, Dad?"

"Alex, you would never believe me." I proceeded to tell her all about the day's events, I finished with telling her about my idea of taking Alex to see Nanny McPhee with Emma Thompson.

"Only you could come up with that idea!" Alex said, as we pulled out of the school car park and headed back to the farm.

CHAPTER 16
THINGS COME TO AN END

A few days later I had contacted the agent of Emma Thompson and the rest is history. Now here I am in the theatre with Emma Thompson with Scarlett and Alex. "How surreal is this?" I was thinking to myself. We all sat and watched the film together. Scarlett was so good, not stirring to be honest. I think she slept through the whole thing. As we said our goodbyes to Emma and her husband at the end of the film, Emma bent down to give Scarlett a cuddle and kissed Alex on the cheek as she left. As we walked out of the theatre, there was still a lot of press around, again there were loads of camera flashes and film crews but as usual Scarlett took it in her stride.

Emma, her husband, and all the stars were getting into cars and heading off to the after-show party. I looked at Alex and Scarlett and said, "Come on girls, let's head home."

Alex gave me a big hug. "Thanks for a great evening, Dad! I will never forget it," she said.

"No! Thank you Alex, I have loved today and glad you were here to share it with me. As we headed back to the car I said to Alex, "Shall we go for one last walk around?"

She replied, "Yes Dad, why not."

We strolled around Trafalgar Square for a while, looking at the fountains. We were getting a few strange looks from a few drunks, who were sitting on the steps, so I thought it best to head back to the car. When we got back to the car, I settled Scarlett into her trailer, gave her a good drink of water and before I had time to hitch the car up to the trailer, I noticed she was fast asleep. Scarlett was not the only one, Alex was fast asleep in the back of the car with her snuggly, it was her blanket which she took on long journeys that helped her to sleep.

We were all hitched up as I pulled slowly out of the car park. I did not know it would be the last time Scarlett and I would come to London! The journey home took about four hours, the roads were very quiet, the night was also very still and dry which was making the journey easy. We pulled up at the farm and I unhitched the trailer, all the time, Scarlett and

Alex were both fast asleep.

"Come on you two," I shouted, and both Scarlett and Alex started to stir.

I watched as both of them walked up to the house side by side, walking in a drunk fashion. I think they were still half asleep. I opened the door, Alex headed to her bed and Scarlett did the same, they were both fast asleep again in seconds. I left the front door open and as I opened the kitchen door, the two dogs bolted through the front. I took them for a quick walk around the field and headed back inside. I settled down in the lounge with Ruby and Cerys, with a strong cup of coffee and thought about the evening. It's not every day you spend an evening with Emma Thompson, I thought and chuckled to myself. Before long I was fast asleep in the arm-chair and heard nothing, until the dogs and Scarlett woke me the next morning.

The next few months saw a lot of changes, one major one, being that Scarlett was getting too big to live in the house, as she was now the size of a large coffee table. She had knocked a few doors off and was breaking things around the house. I was going to have to build her a house in the garden and make her a run with strong fencing; time to call my friends in again to build the fencing. Before long the run was finished and I had built her a large pig house with loads of room for her to stretch out.

I moved Scarlett's toys into her new house, with some apples. Scarlett followed me into the run for a look around and settled down with her teddy bear she had. I sat down with her. It was a very sad time and started to cry as I cuddled her but I knew I had no choice as she was so big. Scarlett seemed to understand, well I hope she did.

Alex came in and sat with us; we were both very sad, things in the house would never be the same again. We had all been sitting in the pig house for fifteen minutes, even the dog had joined us now. I turned to Alex, "Come on we had better go inside and have some tea." We got up and moved out of the run, I left the gate open to see what Scarlett would do. A few minutes later I went outside to check on her and she was fast asleep in her straw. I quietly closed the gate and went back inside.

It was now November 2010 and the weather turned for the worse, it ended up being the coldest winter in years. It started to snow towards the end of November and the snow stayed till the end of December. This made it easy to keep the pig houses clean as the ground was so hard. The major problem we had was all the automatic water feeders had frozen as the temperature never got above minus seven for weeks. Alex and I were having to take buckets of water out to the pigs and other animals twice a day. Alex would fill the buckets in the kitchen and bring them to the back door where I would collect them. We were taking out sixty buckets, twice a day which was a real slog.

Luckily we had plenty of hay, straw and feed for all the animals, as nothing was moving up the road. At first Alex and I loved the weather as we were snowed in and Alex could not get to school in Shrewsbury. After a few weeks we both started to get bored with the weather.

The feed price for the pigs went through the roof. Over a short time the price had gone up by forty pounds a ton. I was buying in sugar beet to lower my food costs. Things were tough as we were not getting any money from our weekend events as nobody could get to us through the winter. Luckily it was our busiest time of the year for pork sales, which kept our heads above water. Spring could not come soon enough, I was thinking and so was Alex.

The weather was affecting our lives and costs of running the farm, and as the snow began to melt we had the problem of the mud. The horses were struggling to move around the paddock and had to spend most of the day in the stables or on the road by the farm when I mucked them out. Things were real tough around the farm and Alex and I were worn out with all the work we had to do and look after all the animals.

Scarlett liked the snow and would run around with the dogs and play in it. The pond was frozen by the farm and Scarlett and the dogs would take themselves off to it and slide across it, which they loved. They would play on it for hours, until the day when it had started to melt and one of the dogs fell through it and I had never seen Ruby move so fast to get out, as she hated the water.

It was hard during this time to keep the house warm. To be honest, Alex and I were getting pretty fed up and not enjoying life as much as we had used to. Life on the farm during the summer is great but during the winter it is hard work and this had been the worst winter since we had been at the farm.

By the time spring came Alex, myself and all the animals looked really fed up. The cost of living on the farm and the feed costs for all the animals had spiralled out of control. I was hoping the feed costs would drop when the spring came but they didn't, they just went up again, I was told it was something to do with the cost of wheat in Russia. It was starting to get worrying with all the expenses, as we had over one hundred and fifty pigs on the farm and loads of other animals that relied on me.

Scarlett was not happy either as she was living on her own which is not the way pigs like to live, they need company. Scarlett was playing with the dogs and me most days but at night she was not happy sleeping on her own. I had a lot of thinking to do.

Alex was also coming to the end of school life as a junior and would soon be going to senior school. She was to go on to Shrewsbury High School for Girls but a lot of her friends were going to Adcote School for Girls, we would have to go and take a look at the school. Alex was also not happy, since living on the farm had not been as much fun as normal and it had been such a tough winter and she was worried about going through another.

It was now February, Alex had been to see Adcote School and had met the Headmaster, Mr Gary Wright, an amazing Head, a larger than life figure. Alex had taken to him and the school which looked like Hogwarts out of Harry Potter, a lovely building set in twenty-four acres of grounds. Alex loved the place and had decided that from September, she wanted to go to Adcote School.

I had come to a decision. I sat Alex down one evening after dinner. "Alex I have had an idea, how about we sell the farm and move!"

"What?" Alex said, "to another farm?"

"No, not to another farm, but a house."

"What! We will not be farming?" she said. "Are you ok with that Dad, what will you do for work?"

"I have found a way I can keep supplying pork without farming."

"What about the animals and Scarlett?"

"I will find them all good homes."

We both grabbed a drink and went for a walk around the farm with the dogs and had a long talk. It was a good two hours later when we got back. We had walked down to the woods and around all the fields, we walked through the patch of Christmas trees we had planted three years ago, which were all about four to five feet tall now. By the time we had got back to the farm-house, we had both decided that this would be the best thing for both of us.

I had a lot to think about. How was I going to find new homes for all the animals? I started to contact a lot of other farmers from the pig farming community and people I had supplied with pigs in the past. I also started to contact a lot of petting farms, where I knew the pigs would not be put to sleep. By now I had seven boars and twenty-four sows, the rest were all growing pigs and piglets for meat and possible breeding. I could not decide what I was going to do with Scarlett, as she was more a pet and would have to be treated as one of the family. As I sat stroking Scarlett, I did not know what to do!

When I started the process, I talked to a few friends of mine who were a great help, especially a guy called Chris, who Alex also knew, as Chris owned a piece of land behind ours. As Chris was into farming, he bought everything that was not bolted down. He even bought Zippy, one of Alex's favourite pigs.

Rose, who was the large Gloucester Old Spot, Alex's first love, went to a petting farm in Somerset. Charlie the British lop boar went off to Ludlow with a couple of sows to a friend of mine. Arthur the Mangalitza boar who was the first pig born on the farm, went to a smallholding down near Cardiff, with a couple of sows. All the boars were found new homes where they would live and breed with other pigs. The same with all the sows, they had all gone off for breeding or to petting farms.

One woman who had come from over the Welsh border bought a British lop boar and two sows, and when she saw the llamas she asked, "What are you doing with them?"

"They are for sale, too." I said.

"I will have them all," she said. It took us three days to catch them all as they are very good at jumping fences. We eventually got them into the stables and when the lady came back with her large trailer, which we backed up to the stables, the llamas walked straight on, with no trouble.

Luckily we had found a home for all the horses, with a friend of Alex's from school, which meant Alex could see them if she wanted to. We also found a good home for the donkeys. All was going well. Chris had bought all the sheep and the chickens, so the farm was getting very quiet.

It was now mid-July and I was remembering waking up one morning and looking out of the window, the sight I would normally see, was pigs strolling around the pens, making all their grunting noises, with the llamas, donkeys and horses walking around in the background. This morning I saw only Scarlett's mum and one other pig called Skippy, just walking around, Scarlett was in the garden. I just stood looking, it was so quiet, and the shock just hit me that nothing would ever be the same and this way of life had ended. A tear fell from the corner of my eye, followed by a flood of tears. I just could not stop crying.

Alex had come into the room and cuddled me. "I know, Dad," Alex said. "I feel the same; let's take the dogs for a walk down to the woods. That will cheer us up."

"Ok, Alex, I will get dressed."

We both grabbed a cup of tea and took the dogs for a walk. As we started to leave, I could hear Scarlett. "Let's take Scarlett!" I said to Alex. At that, Alex ran off through the garden. The next minute Scarlett came running through the gate. We all went for a long walk and enjoyed every minute of it. I never knew at the time but this would be the last time we all went on a walk together.

The very next day a man turned up to pick up Scarlett's mum and Zippy. While I was helping Mark load the pigs, I was talking to him and his wife about Scarlett and being the last pig to find a home.

"Can we have a look at her?" Mark's wife said.

"Yes! No problem." We walked into the garden and I let Scarlett out. Scarlett took to Mark's wife straight away.

"Oh can we have her?" she said to Mark.

"As long as you understand she is a pet and not a normal pig, then you can have her."

We walked Scarlett around to the back of the trailer and as we started to load her, the dogs seemed to know what was happening. Scarlett turned and ran back to the dogs and they all licked each other. Scarlett took a long look back at the house and the trampoline; I looked too and thought that is where it all started two years ago. As Scarlett came back she nuzzled up against my leg, I bent down and gave her a large hug.

I was now on my knees and could not stop myself from crying. Scarlett moved her face against mine and I felt a tear come down her face onto mine, Scarlett seemed to know she was leaving and this would be the last time she would see the farm. I stood up and Scarlett followed me onto the trailer.

As we shut the doors, I turned to Mark, "Can I bring Alex over to say her goodbyes?"

"Yes sure, no problem," Mark said. Scarlett was only moving fifteen minutes down the road to Anscroft.

As they left, I closed the top gate behind them and turned to walk back towards the house, looking at all the empty pens as I walked back. This was so hard and felt my heart being wrenched out of me.

I went into the farmhouse, made a cup of tea and took the dogs for a walk and spent the next hour walking around the fields and taking a trip down memory lane. I thought to myself everything happens for a reason but for the life of me, I could not think what it was.

I picked Alex up from school later that day and drove over to Anscroft. "Why are we going over here?" she asked.

"You are going to say goodbye to Scarlett, her mum and Zippy," which was Alex's favourite pig.

Alex started to cry. "Come on," I said. "Chin up, Scarlett has gone to a good home and we knew this day was coming." As we arrived at Mark's place, I gave Alex a *pig hug* before we got out of the car. We met Mark and his wife and walked over to where Scarlett was. As Scarlett saw Alex, she ran over to her barking like a dog. Alex went into her pen and we left them alone together for about half an hour.

I went back outside to find Alex. As I went into the pen, I found Alex inside the pig house hugging Scarlett and talking to her. "How are you both doing?" I said climbing into the pen. We both sat either side of Scarlett talking and hugging her. "Come on, Alex," I said, "we had better be heading home."

"Ok Dad, I am quite hungry, what's for dinner?"

"Kid's cottage pie," I said.

"Mmmm… yum, yum," Alex said.

As we left, we both looked back at Scarlett's pen, she was standing up on the corner of the fence and watched us leave. Alex and I said nothing all the way home. We were both in shock and had a good cry and a hug when we arrived back at the farm. We had luckily found a buyer for the farm as Alex and I both agreed; we did not want to be there any more, now all the animals had gone. We had sold a lot of the land off separately and the farm had been sold with five acres of land.

It was about a month later when the day had come to leave the farm. Anything that could be sold outside and around the farm was gone. The whole place looked so empty and sad. As the last items were loaded onto the van, I turned to Alex. "Are you ready?"

"Can I have a last look at my bedroom?" she asked.

"Yes, of course you can, just close the door behind you when you come out." I went down to the removal men and told them we would meet up at the new house. I confirmed they had the address, and as they left, I could hear Alex walking up behind me. "Ok, Dad I am ready, let's go."

As we started to drive away, I stopped the car and we both looked back. Alex looked at me, "This is where we were a few years ago, do you remember, the first time you brought me to look at the farm?"

"Yes, I do! That was a long time ago." We hugged again and shed a few more tears.

"Come on, let's go. Dad, where are the dogs?"

"Oh! Knickers! In the garden, ha ha ha." We shot back

to the farm, loaded the dogs and headed off.

CHAPTER 17
WHERE ARE WE NOW?

It is now September and we are living in the small town of Wem. Alex had wanted to stay outside of Shrewsbury. It is a lovely small market town, a quiet sleepy village not far from Alex's new school. So what are we up to now? Well....

Alex is at her new school called Adcote. An amazing place set in twenty-six acres of lovely grounds. She settled well into year seven, and has decided she wants to be a vet, which will be great if she does. Alex also likes all three sciences and finds maths easy, so that would be a help. It is her call at the end of the day, and being at Adcote would help Alex on her way. Alex has become a bit of a book worm; where ever she goes her head is in a book, reading a book a week. It was the Twilight books that got her into reading which is great as Alex hardly goes onto the internet, except to read a book. She does make me smile. Alex has made a lot of friends at the school and is a popular member of the class. Alex could not be happier.

What is Scarlett up to you may ask? Well, she is ruling the roost at Mark's place. Scarlett lives on the back field behind Mark's house. Scarlett lives in a large pig house and has her first ever boyfriend. He is called Delboy and is a large Gloucester Old Spot Boar. Scarlett bosses him around and makes sure he does not look at another female pig. Alex and I have been over to see her and she has not forgotten us. Scarlett would come over and give us a hug. After about ten minutes she would go off back to her boyfriend Delboy. I looked at Alex. "I think she has settled in well, she does not really want to know us now." We laughed and walked off together back to the car. As we left, we looked back to see her playing with Delboy, in their large field. We looked at each other, smiled and drove off. Pigs can live for twenty years, so I think she will live a happy life over in Anscroft.

And me, well I am taking my private pilot's licence (PPL); yes I am learning to fly a plane. For some reason I can't find anyone who has agreed to come up with me when I have passed and can take passengers. Even Alex does not want to come up with me; I don't know why! I have had a few lessons and this is the day when I take my first solo flight. I am sitting in the two seater, Cessna 152; I have done all my pre-flight checks and am waiting at the end of the runway. I am waiting for the air tower to tell me I can go. I was having a lot to think about, as every other time I have flown the instructor has been there to put me right. Another plane lands and taxies down and off to the right. I have been given clearance to take off. I head off down the runway picking up speed; as I go past the air tower, I wave while pulling back on the stick with one hand. I am sure I could see them shaking their heads as I flew past them. I started to gain altitude. I thought to myself now, "Mmmm...what did he say about landing? OH CRAP!"

CHAPTER 18
JANUARY 2017

I wrote this book three years ago, which covered a period up to 2011. I have added these updated details to the book so you know where we are as of January 2017.

Alex is now nearly 16, and has done well at her school Adcote. Alex tends to have a go at most sports. Across the board Alex does well with them all. Not as interested in running like she used to be, but a demon in the pool. I used to let Alex take a few strides before we started a race in the pool. Always, I would just about win; when I think back, how it has changed. Even if Alex gave me a few lengths head start I would still lose to her. If I say something mad such as 'let's race over four lengths', I get lapped. I can't quite believe it.

As I look back over the past four years, so many things have changed with Alex. She wanted to be a vet for a long time but that has now changed completely. Alex is a lover of books, she cannot get enough of them, and reading teen fiction is her passion. Alex also has an Instagram account and is a blogger, as they call it. Not quite sure how it all works as technology is not my thing. What I mean is, I love everything about it, it amazes me, but I do not understand it and have trouble using it too. Alex blogs about the books she reads reviewing them, making videos and having over 4,000 followers. Alex now has authors sending her books to review, bookmarks and other items come like executive candles.

Alex has an amazing knack for making films of her to blog. She is also doing amazingly well at drama getting distinctions and finds performing on stage very easy, expressing herself well. Last year Alex won a trophy at Adcote for the best performer in drama throughout the whole school. Alex now will be going onto sixth form, taking A level English, sociology, film and drama. She wants to get a job in broadcast journalism at the BBC; knowing Alex she will get there in the end, being in front of the camera performing or behind the camera directing.

As for Scarlett, you may ask what she has been up to. As you know, Scarlett went to live on a friend's farm near to Shrewsbury. Scarlett lived out her years bossing Delboy around. This was a Gloucester old spot boar that she took a shine to when arriving at the farm and immediately moved into his pig ark. Scarlett made herself at home on the farm not just bossing him around but all the other pigs on the farm. Scarlett used to take herself off for walks down to a neighbour's farm. Scarlett would find her way into his veg patch eating all of his strawberries. When I was told about this on one of my visits, I had to have a chuckle thinking, 'yep, that's Scarlett, has a mind of her own'. Every time Alex and I went to visit Scarlett, she would remember us and come bounding across the field towards us barking like a dog.

Scarlett soon became a character in the farming locality, always breaking out of the field she was in. She'd be found walking down the road or in someone's garden eating them out of house and home. The last time we went to visit her, Scarlett was showing her years; we saw her lying under a tree on a hot day fast asleep. Scarlett did not even hear us walking towards her until we were next to her. As Alex knelt down to stroke her, she jumped with a start.

"Oh Scarlett, I'm sorry, did I scare you?" Alex said.

We spent a good hour with her, stroking her and talking about the funny times we had with her. As we left, Scarlett was dozing under the tree. We looked back at her and then at each other. I think we both realised that this was the last time we would see her. We carried on walking.

"Alex, I'm just going back for a minute. See you at the car."

"Ok, Dad, see you there."

I turned and walked back to Scarlett who stood up to greet me. I could not help myself; I started to cry thinking of what we had done together. As I moved closer, I could see a tear come from her eye, which never happens as pigs cannot do that normally. As I sat next to her, she nuzzled into me and let out a big sigh. Scarlett lay her head down across my lap as I stroked and talked to her. I think even Scarlett knew this was the last time we would see each other.

As I sat with her, she rolled over for a belly rub. "Wow Scarlett, I've not done this in ages!" I said to her.

A big smile came over her face as I rub rubbed, letting out the occasional squeal, which brought back memories of when Scarlett was living in the house lying on the sofa next to me having belly rubs. 'Where had the years gone', I thought.

Delboy had already passed away and apparently Scarlett was missing him loads. I sat for a few moments more before getting up to leave. As I did I said, 'love you Scarlett'. She barked back at me.

As I walked down the hill, the tears were rolling down my face uncontrollably. I turned for one last look. I could see

Scarlett was still standing, craning her neck to see me till the last minute. I got back to the car and hugged Alex. The very next morning we had a phone call from my friend telling me Scarlett had died that night in her sleep but before she had passed away, Scarlett had managed to enter the veg patch, eating more strawberries from the garden.

I took Alex to school and drove over to the farm. As I walked into Scarlett's house, I found her curled up in the corner. I had given Scarlett a teddy bear years ago when she lived with us. Scarlett always slept with it. As I went over to her, I could see that between her legs, she had snuggled into her teddy bear; maybe Scarlett was thinking about me before she went to sleep. I like to think so.

We carefully took Scarlett and her teddy to her favourite wood where we buried them together. It was another place she liked to go for walks when we lived on the farm. Scarlett was about 8 when she left for pastures new and greener. I will never forget Scarlett and feel my life is the better for her being a part of it.

And where am I? Well, if you remember I was just taking off in a plane for my first solo flight around the airfield and yes I landed the plane ok, well I thought so. After the next solo flight, I had to give up learning to fly as I had a feeling that maybe my life was in peril. Let me tell you what happened the next time when flying solo.

I was sitting at the end of the runway in the Sena152 airplane, waiting for the go ahead to take off. "That's it, I've got it!"

They had told me to go and off I did go, belting down the runway with a smile on my face. I was looking all around me and into the air I went. It felt like I was flying in the battle of Britain, heading off with my squadron. I chuckled and thought, 'what am I like'. After a while, I started to daydream and thought I would go over towards Welshpool, follow the A458. Thirty minutes had gone by; I had heard nothing over the radio and I did not recognise anything.

"Oh crap, what's that lake?" I said out loud. Still talking out loud to myself, "Oh no, that's Bala Lake...how the hell have I ended up here? Why haven't I heard anything over the radio?" I said.

Oh crap, I had pulled the radio connection out without knowing. I plugged it back in and straight away I heard a guy shouting my number out. I replied and said sorry, for some reason the radio had not been working. Well, I wasn't going to tell them what I had done.

"Where are you?" came the voice.

"Well, ummm, I'm over by Bala Lake," I said.

"You're where???" came the reply in a high pitched voice.

I nearly started to laugh but thought better of it. "I'm over Bala Lake; it's lovely over here, blue sky."

The voice stopped me in my tracks. "I don't care what the weather is like, get yourself back to the airfield. It's getting late."

I put the plane into a steep turn and headed back, hopefully the way I had come. I was looking for landmarks to reassure me that I was going the right way but nothing did, until I saw Chirk Castle, which I had flown over many times before. I had gone a bit wayward but knew my way back from here. Only problem I had now was it was starting to get dark. I thought, 'let's go as fast as I can'.

Now flying flat out, the tower came over the radio asking me where I was with a worried tone to their voice.

"I'm about ten minutes away," I said. Hopefully that was Shrewsbury ahead of me, I thought.

"How much fuel have you got?" they asked.

Hmmm, I had not thought of that. I looked. OMG I was on empty!

"Erhhhhh, yes seems to be pretty low," I said.

They went quiet. Still looking for Shrewsbury, I said to

myself, 'yes it's Shrewsbury' and there was the road I knew that headed towards the airfield. I followed it, flying lower than usual as it was getting dark. At one point I was following a car's headlights. I was thinking maybe I could land the plane on the road. Hmmm, maybe not.

'Yeah'! I said to myself. 'I've made it, there's the air tower'. At that, the plane started to splutter. 'Oh, pooh', I said, sinking into my seat. I told the Tower I was running out of fuel and was coming straight in.

All I heard on the other end was someone saying, "Oh, crap Steve's coming in. The plonker's run out of fuel."

'How unfair', I thought. 'It's not my fault'. I did not have enough time to fly round the Tower as normal. Heading for the wrong end of the runway was my only option. I was coming in fast and steeper than normal. The sweat was pouring off me. I was gripping the stick tightly, looking all around me, not sure what I was looking for really. The Tower was shouting, 'pull back, slow down'. I'm sure I heard someone say, 'what a bloody wally'. They were really having a go at me. 'Well, here goes', I said as I came in a full speed, trying to pull back on the stick but it was too late. Instead of a nice soft landing, I came in and pancaked the plane. Well, that's what they call it. I came in so hard I snapped the under-carriage. The wheels went flying in all directions, and the plane skid across the runway on the its belly and came to a stop.

Wow, the fire engine was coming towards me with lights flashing. People were running towards me. 'This is so cool, just like in the movies', I thought.

I opened the door shouting, 'don't worry, I'm fine. All ok here'. No one seemed to be happy with me.

I went for a cup of tea and a private meeting with my instructor with him asking me, did I really want to fly? I got the drift of the meeting and had to agree they were probably right, and I should stick to being a passenger.

After that, the last few years have been pretty normal. The line of work I have been doing is helping people save money in a greener way which is cool. I spent a few years writing this book, also working with hotels. Alex and I now live in Shrewsbury with our Dalmatian Ruby. We both like our new home as it's within walking distance to the town centre.

We've spent time down in Cornwall, going for walks along the coast exploring new places and looking for new adventures. We couldn't be happier.

'Do we miss the farm'? you may be thinking. I miss some of the things, like the way of life (even though hard), the animals and the good friends who helped me. What we do not miss is the hard winters. They were so much hard work. I take my hat off to farmers in the winter. Their job is so hard.

I am hoping to have a large fireworks party this year. Wow, you should see how many fireworks I've already got. It should be a blast. Literally. Some of them fire off 1000 rockets. I can't wait! I know, it says stand 20 metres away, but I'm sure putting them all a foot apart will do. Hmmm, I've just realised when setting them off, I will be only a few feet away. Oh, well!

THE END

IN SUPPORT OF:

A percentage of the proceeds of sales go to a charity called
Children Today.

www.childrentoday.org.uk

Children Today raises funds to provide specialised equipment and
services for children and young people with disabilities
throughout the UK.

Children Today was founded in 1994 to help disabled children and
young people up to the age of 25 enjoy a better quality of life by
providing them with the specialised equipment they need.

Often children and young people with disabilities remain excluded
from a lifestyle which other people may take for granted. They
want to join in and take part in the same sorts of activities, within
their capabilities, as other children. They want to gain more
independence from their parents as they get older, but are
often prevented from doing so.

This charity is close to my heart as I was born with a disability and
I know how difficult things can be for families going through this.

ACKNOWLEDGEMENTS

My daughter Alex who is always in my corner.
Alex is my reason why.

Frieda Hughes; friends don't get any better than this. Thank you
for your support. I would never have written this book without it.

Peter, who was my closest friend whilst going through my teens –
thanks for the fun memories.

A big thanks goes out to Tommy, Andy and Chris for all their help
around the farm.

Sue Miller, my editor from TeamAuthorUK for polishing my book
and making it that little bit more special.

Illustrator Alan Jones for the amazing cover designs, even when he
only had a scrap of an idea to work with.

ABOUT THE AUTHOR

Stephen Howell was born in Shrewsbury Shropshire, after a varied career working in far-off places.

Stephen now resides back in his home town with his daughter Alex and their dog Ruby. He has never been shy in coming forward with everything he does. When not writing, he enjoys walking the hills of Shropshire or finding new adventures around the Cornish coast and further afield. His other pleasures are curling up in front of a roaring fire watching a good movie.

Scarlett The Pig is his debut novel, which is a true story set over two years. It follows the lives of Steve, his daughter Alex and their trampolining pig, Scarlett.

'This is where I spent two summers writing the book. Thank you to the Corn Mill at Llangollen for accommodating me, also thanks for supplying me with loads of tea and great food plus an amazing back-drop.'

To see what Steve's next project is, go to:

www.stevehowellauthor.com

F: @stevehowellauthor

T: @stevehowellauthor

Follow Alex Howell on Instagram:

alexxhowelll

69342444R00120

Made in the USA
Columbia, SC
17 April 2017